Motobu Choki

本部朝基

My Karate Jutsu

私の唐手術

Translated by

ERIC SHAHAN

Translator's Introduction

This book reprints Motobu Choki's 1932 book and provides an English translation on the following page. His book includes many photographs showing how to do techniques correctly.

Some additional illustrations have been included from contemporary sources to supplement the explanations. These additional illustrations will all be labeled with the source.

In addition, at the end of this book a collection of articles related to Motobu Choki have been included that were not part of Motobu Choki's original book.

This book was originally intended for a mainland Japanese audience so many terms that would have been read differently in the Ryuku language have been changed for the mainland Japanese audience. In addition there is some internal inconsistency with how terms are rendered in Japanese. The transcriptions of names and places reflects how the publisher chose to render them.

In addition, Japanese underwent a revision following world war II meaning the way the Kana alphabet is used was changed. For example the word Okinawa 沖縄 is given the reading of おきなは which would seem to indicate the name is read "Okinaha." However, in pre-war Japanese the Kana は was often used instead of わ to indicate "wa." Similarly in the era Motobu Choki wrote this book the Kana くわ appear to indicate "Kuwa" however this would actually be "Ka" and is today rendered with the Kana か.

Table of Contents

目次

Table of Contents

目次

私の唐手術・MY KARATE JUTSU

本部朝基・MOTOBU CHOKI

Watashi no Karate Jutsu
By Motobu Choki

Introductory Calligraphy by Baron Oi

尚武

陸軍大将
男爵大井成元題

陸軍大将勳一等功一級從二位男爵

貴族院議員　大井成元閣下題字

Introductory Calligraphy by Baron Oi

Transcript of calligraphy	Army General Baron Oi Shigemoto (1863 ~ 1951)
尚武 陸軍大将 男爵大井成元題	

Respect for martial valor and skills.
Introductory Calligraphy by
Oi Shigemoto

Awards

1896 - Order of the Sacred Treasure, 6th class
1896 - Order of the Golden Kite, 5th class
1914 - Order of the Sacred Treasure, 2nd class
1919 - Grand Cordon of the Order of the Sacred Treasure
1920 - Grand Cordon of the Order of the Rising Sun
1920 - Order of the Golden Kite, 1st class

Photograph of the author Motobu Choki

醫學上より觀たる唐手

「治療よりも豫防」と言ふ標語は、輓近保健衛生上最も合理的のものと唱道せられてゐる。此の標語に基きて、疾病を完全に豫防せんと欲せば、須らく身體を強健にし、而して病毒に對する抵抗力を增進せしむるにあるは勿論である。

衛生法には幾多の種類がある。其の中に於て、最も樞要にして體育養生上に大影響を釀すものは、實に筋肉の運動である。是れ、專ら筋骨の發達を促し、身體の基礎を鞏固にするからである。

今諸種の運動法中、其の適否を撰擇吟味するは、頗る緊要の件であつて、又極めて困難なる問題である。然し之れを要するに、其軀幹四肢共に平等の動作を營爲するや、將又一部の筋骨にのみ影響するやを的確に定るにあると思ふ、則ち全身の筋肉發達が平衡を保ち、茲に始めて健康の體格と稱することが出來る。一局部の筋肉のみの運動に偏倚すれば、生理上の均衡を失し、其結果畸形の體格に變ずるの恐れがある。

私は、以上の如き運動生理上の原則に立脚し、且つ體質の改善と新陳代謝の促進に關する知見とを對比し、倂せて武士道鼓吹をも考慮するに、目下流行する諸種の運動方法中、最も優秀にして理

Karate from a medical perspective
By Doctor of Medicine Toguchi Seiko

Toguchi Seiko (1881~1959.) Born in Naha
沖縄県人物風景写真大観
Photographs of People and Places in Okinawa Prefecture
1935

Recently, health experts have been almost universal in promoting the phrase "prevention before treatment" as the most reasonable approach to staying healthy. The fundamental meaning of this phrase is, if you want to prevent illness, you need a strong body. It goes without saying, but as your body becomes stronger, you become more resistant to disease.

There are a multitude of ways to make a healthy body. However, amongst them, the one that will have the greatest effect on your health is exercising the muscles of your body. What I am referring to is focusing on developing all your sinews and muscles in order to stiffen the core of your body.

There are a great many methods of exercise out there, and while choosing the best one is crucial, it can also be a vexing decision. I believe there are basically two choices you can make: Either choose a system that allows you to manipulate your core and limbs evenly and in unison, or a system that focuses on one point of the body so it can move precisely. Clearly, a system that allows you to develop the muscles in every part of your body evenly and maintains that development will enable you to achieve a healthy body.

二

想的なるは唐手の右に出ずるものは無いと斷言して憚らないのである。況んや、其の姿勢と威容の整備と質習し易い事とは、實に他の運動法が追隨を許さない特徵があるに於てをやである。尚ほ更に膽力養成上に神益する點は、一層の光彩を添へるの觀がある。私は唐手を以て强ち、闘爭の具のみに歸し度くない。又一地方的のものに止め度くない。專ら之れを體育向上に善用し、全日本民族否全世界の男女に對し、此唐手を擴張普及し、以て世界的に發達せしめ、而して現今保健衛生上の缺陷を補充し、萎靡せる體格を改造せられん事を希望するものである。

時恰も斯道の蘊奧を極めたる達人本部朝基氏の「私の唐手術」と題する著書を公にし、其技術を闡明ならしめたるを聞き、國家の爲め雙手を擧げて養成推奬するものである。尚ほ此企圖に對し、天下同好の士の共鳴せらるゝを疑はないのである。私は此古き歷史を有する唐手が、單に運動界に貢献するのみならず、更に進んで精神敎育上にも亦多大の效果を齎すものなる事を期待するものである。爲に聊か上記の如き所感を叙して以て序文と爲す。

昭和七年二月廿日

醫學博士　渡　口　精　鴻

On the other hand, by only training the muscles of one part of the body, muscle development in your body will become unbalanced. There is a risk that this imbalance could cause the muscles of your body to become misaligned or even deformed.

Up to this point, I have introduced the principles of healthy exercise. However, while improving the state of your body and rejuvenating your metabolism are important, we must also consider promoting Bushido, the Samurai mindset.

Looking at the many popular methods of exercise that can be found today, I can say unequivocally and without hesitation that no other method is more ideally suited to this task than the well-developed system of Karate. Whether you are looking at the Karate stances, the dignified way all the parts of the body are carefully positioned or the ease of practice, its particular nature seems to dictate it will not allow any other method of exercise to surpass it.

Further, the fact that Karate training also serves to develop your courage only increases its brilliance. However, I do not wish to categorize Karate simply as a tool to strengthen the body before going into battle. At the same time, do I wish to have it considered to be an art limited to one region of the world. I wish to see it adapted as a method of physical fitness that is not only practiced by the people of Japan, but by men and women all over the world. It is my hope that expanding Karate teaching globally will result in an increase in the overall physical fitness level of all people. This will serve to surmount unhealthy practices as it helps people to develop their shrunken forms.

Recently a man who has developed a thorough understanding of all aspects of this art, Motobu Choki, has decided to release a book titled *My Karate Jutsu*, to the public. I have heard that the techniques are explained clearly, so I raise both hands as I give my full throated approval of this contribution to Japanese society. Clearly this book has my strongest recommendation. I have no doubt that all those who follow the path of Karate will be overjoyed at this publication. As for myself, I am pleased that Karate, with its long history, will not only contribute to the world of exercise, but I also anticipate it will be effective as a method of teaching people how to strengthen their minds.

With these few words I have outlined my feelings in this preface.

-February 20th of Showa 7 (1932)

序

時代の浪が、大きく荒れてゐる。

理想に生きんとする者も、現實に生きる者も凡てが、闘爭に等しい日常生活を生活してゐる。

強く、明るく、淸い生活が標榜される。

そのためには、鞏固な意志と、勇氣と壯健な肉體とが要求される。

唐手の存在意義も、實に其處にある。

斯界の大家、本部朝基先生に待つこと極めて多きものゝ今日あることは今更喋々を要せぬ。

今、本書の世に出づるを聞き、衷心、喜びに堪えぬ。

唐手の存在意義が一人でも多くの世の同志に理解され、之を通じて明るい、正しい世界へと凡て

が歴史の車を押し進めるため、協同參加されんことを切に希望して止まぬ。

昭和七年三月九日

早稻田大學唐手研究會々長

杉 山 謙 治

16

Foreword
President of the Waseda University Karate Research Society
Sugiyama Keiji

Sugiyama Keiji (1898~1948)
Japan Education Innovation Declaration
日本教育革新宣言 1944

The waves rocking our era are both large and rough.

Both those that are trying to live by ideals and those that are trying to live in reality are now finding themselves living life as if they are in a state of war.

They are advocating for a strong, bright and clean life.

To have that requires being brave, being firm in your intent, and having a strong and healthy body.

The fact is the essence of Karate lies here.

The degree to which innumerable great Karate practitioners are awaiting Motobu Choki Sensei' book cannot be overstated.

As for myself, I was beside myself with joy when I heard this book was going to be made available to the public. My hope is if even one more person can be made aware of the principles of Karate, people all over the world can understand each other. That connection can serve as a driving force to forge a bright new era for the world, I am extremely excited by the prospects of future cooperation.

-March 9th of Showa 7 (1932)

はしがき

私は、嘗て大正十五年の春、唐手術宣傳の爲め、パンフレットを發行したことがあつた。其後僅か數年、識者の理解ある同情と研究家諸君の不斷の努力は、唐手研究熱を急激に勃興せしめ、今や全國的なものに迄ならしめんとしてゐる、斯道の爲め誠に喜ばしき次第である。

亦最近社會生活の困難は、或は青年學生を無氣力にし、文弱に流れしめ或は亦其言行徒に過激に走らしめるものがあるが、之は誠に憾歎すべきことであつて、かゝる際、尚武精神を隆にし、以て質實剛健の氣風を養ふことは極めて必要なことであつて、是れ社會に一面武士道鼓吹熱の盛んなる所以である。

今私が、既に二三の好著あるにも拘はらず、且つ亦身の淺學菲才をも顧みず、此處に筆を執るのは唐手術の眞髄を示し、更に此の機運を促進せしめん爲めであつて、若し大方諸彦の賛同を得れば筆者無上の光榮とする處である。

本書の出版に際して、多大の配慮と援助に與つた漢那朝常君、亦殊に題字揮與の榮を賜はつた男爵大井成元大將閣下、序文の勞を執られた渡口精鴻博士、杉山謙治教授に對しては衷心より感謝の意を表す。

昭和七年三月　　著　者　誌

Preface
Motobu Choki

In the spring of the 15th year of the Taisho Emperor (1926) I published a pamphlet[1] to promote Karate Jutsu. In the handful of years since then, thanks to the understanding of experts in the field and the relentless investigation of researchers, passion for Karate training has suddenly exploded, resulting in Karate being practiced all over Japan. This brings me a deep sense of joy.

The reason is, one problem affecting society is a certain lack of vitality amongst the youth. They seem to be swept away by entertaining books. While at the same time the way they talk and act grow more and more extreme. This is a perilous state of affairs. It is essential that we foster a martial spirit in order to instill a truly fierce sense of mission in the youth of today.

This is the reason that Bushido, the spirit of the Samurai, is being encouraged in parts of society these days. Though I am hardly an academic and there are already two or three good books on Karate already available this book I have penned contains the essence of Karate Jutsu which I hope will further encourage the spread of Karate. Nothing would please me more than if the great practitioners were to look favorably upon this work.

There are many people who were kind enough to offer their assistance in getting this book published. I would like to thank Kanna Chojo for his assistance as well as army general His Excellency Baron Oi Shigemoto for the fantastic introductory calligraphy. I was honored to receive forewords from both doctor Toguchi Seiko and Sugiyama Keiji and I offer them my humble thanks.

-March of Showa 7 (1932)

---

[1] Motobu Choki uses the English word "pamphlet" to describe his first book *Karate Jutsu: Kumite*.

私の唐手術

本部朝基

唐手の意義と起源

琉球、即ち沖縄に於ては、古來一種靈妙な武術が存在し、汎く縣下に普及されて居る。これ拳闘術に非ず、柔術にあらず、それらに似て、而も全然趣きを異にし、獨自の境地を行く唐手即ち空手である。それは徒手空拳、身に寸鐵を帶びすして、突く、打つ、蹴るの三方法を利用して、一撃よく敵を挫き、一蹴よく凶暴を制し、以て護身の用を全うし、安寧生存を確保する武術である。

一代の英雄ナポレオンをして、武器の無い東洋の一小國として驚嘆せしめたのは、是の唐手國沖縄である。

この靈妙至極なる唐手術は、何時の頃より、沖縄に行はれて居たかに就いては、種々の說があるが、確たる文献

一

My Karate Jutsu
The Origin and Meaning of Karate
Motobu Choki

In Ryukyu, now called Okinawa, there is a wonderful type of martial art that has been passed down from days of old and is practiced all over the prefecture. It is neither boxing, nor is it Jujutsu. In fact, the entire substance of the art differs and it is on its own plateau. What I am talking about is called *Karate* 唐手 Chinese Hand or *Kuhte* 空手 empty hand.

It is a type of *Toshu Kuhken* 徒手空拳 bare handed and empty handed fighting technique. Without so much as a Suntetsu,[2] you instead rely on three methods: Tsuki, thrusting, Uchi, hitting and Keri, Kicking.

With one attack you can topple your opponent and with one kick you can bring a villain under control. In short, this martial art allows you to protect yourself while also maintaining peace and tranquility.

The once in a lifetime warrior Emperor Napoleon was left thunderstruck when he heard there was a small nation in the Pacific whose inhabitants carried no weapons. That was the Karate nation of Okinawa.

2

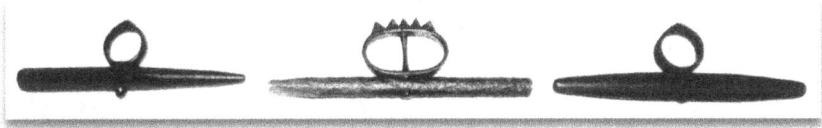

Examples of 19th century Suntetsu 寸鉄 from unknown schools. This is a close-quarters self-defense weapon that means "close iron."

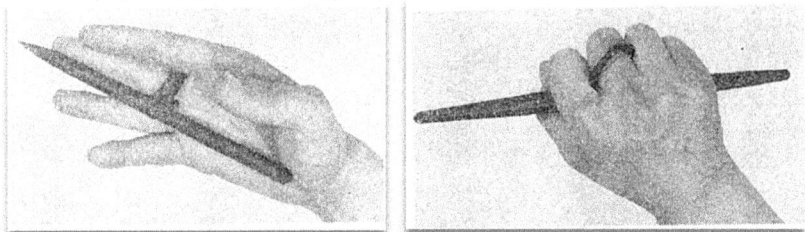

Demonstrating the Suntetsu, Nawa Yukio *Hidden Weapons* 1977.

二

がない爲、判然してゐない。元來、唐手は、釋迦二十七世の法孫達磨太子が印度より遙々梁の國に至り、武帝と

意合はす、去つて、魏の國に赴き、小林寺に入り、見性強身の説を立て、子弟の體育的精神的鍛練の爲に創案教

授せられたるに、其の源を發してゐる。これが代々傳はり、支那古來の武術と合し、小林寺派拳法となり、他

派と離れて獨自の拳法の分野を副してきた。其の琉球に入つたのは、慶長後島津家の琉球禁武制策と、四圍の事

情より、琉球在來の武術と合し、取捨撰擇洗練の結果、唐手として隆々發達を遂げたものと思はれる。

Due to the lack of documentation, it is impossible to determine when the marvelous Karate Jutsu techniques began to be practiced in Okinawa, though there are many theories.

The traditional story is that the Bodhidharma, a Buddhist monk who lived during the 5th or 6th century AD, and the 27th successor of the Gautama Buddha. Dharma traveled from India to distant Liang dynasty China where he met with Emperor Wu.[3] Leaving there, he headed to Northern Wei and took up residence at the Shorinji Temple. There he developed the concept of *Misei Kyoshin* 見性強身 Discern your essence and develop all parts of your body.

The start of Karate was when the Dharma developed a new program for the students at the temple that would forge not only the mind, but the body as well. Beginning from that point in ancient China these techniques were then passed down to generation after generation.

They merged with other martial arts and eventually the Shorinji Temple style moved away from the other styles and established its own distinct style of Kenpo. These techniques are thought to have come to the Ryukyu islands sometime after the Keicho era (1596 ~ 1615,) when the Shimazu clan passed an ordinance banning weapons in the Ryukyu islands. From the best information available, it seems these techniques were merged with the native martial arts of Ryukyu. These techniques were refined by keeping what was good about each system and abandoned what was not. From there, Karate began to flourish and achieve renown.

---

[3] Regarding Emperor Wu's meeting with the Dharma:

According to Buddhist tradition, Bodhidharma, the first Zen patriarch of China, came to visit Emperor Wu around 520. The emperor told Bodhidharma that he had built temples and given financial support to the monastic community, and asked the patriarch how much merit he had gained for these actions. Bodhidharma replied, "None whatsoever." Perplexed, the emperor then asked the eminent monk who he was to tell him such things, to which he answered, "I know not." Bodhidharma then left the imperial court to continue his travels throughout China.

-Seeing Through Zen
John R. McRae, 2003

琉球における唐手の系統

古來、琉球に傳はれる唐手は首里・那覇・泊の三系統に大別することが出來る。尤もそれは流儀が異なるといふ意味でなく、習練者の體質、その他の關係より、各教授師範の方法を異にし、それが長い間の傳統となつて、傳はり來たつたのである。

古來、首里に於ては、稽古の初期は、六分の力をもつて習練し、ひたすら敏活を旨とした。那覇に於ては、それと反對に、十分の力を傾注して、專ら、筋骨の發達に意を用ひた。泊に至つては、首里・那覇と趣きを異にし、一風變つた系統を傳へ來たつたものである。廢藩前まで、泊港は琉球の第二貿易港であつたため、屢々支那・朝鮮等より、通交船が漂着することがあつた。それが爲め、此の地には是等漂着者の群を收容すべき客舍を設け、琉球國王の命によつて、漂着者をここで歡待してゐたのである。從つて、長い年月の間には、泊の村人はその客舍に出入し、漂着者の群に加はつて居る武人より、唐手の傳授をうけ、茲に泊獨特の拳法が發生したのである。

然るに、上述の事を辨へずして、後人これが爲に説をなし、これを琉球に傳はる唐流儀であると誤り傳へ、且つ、その基本姿勢までも、根本から異る様に流布するも、基本姿勢は、何れの場合も八文字立で、力の入れ方、足の扱ひ方など、總て同一で、その間少しも差異なく、何れも一得一失あれど、稽古者はただ敏活を期することが肝要である。

Karate Lineages in Ryukyu

Traditionally, the Karate transmitted in the Ryukyu islands can be divided into three main categories: Shuri, Naha and Tomari. However, this does not mean that there are different teaching traditions. Rather, it refers to both the differences in body type of the early practitioners as well as the training methodology used by each instructor. Over a long period of time, these methods became established practices and these traditions were passed on to later generations.

From long ago, Shuri style training would initially consist of using sixty percent power when training, meaning they focused on speed and agility.

The Naha style is the opposite. Naha style practitioners always put a hundred percent of power into strikes. They focus exclusively on developing the muscles and sinews of the body.

Tomari style, on the other hand is different in substance, from both Naha and Shuri styles due to its unconventional origins. Before the Meiji government began replacing the feudal domain with prefectures, Tomari harbor was known as the second great trading port of the Ryukyu Islands. Because of this trading ships from China or the Korean Peninsula would frequently drift into the harbor.[4] In response to this, a facility was constructed to house the crew of the ships that had been adrift. The king of the Ryukyu Islands personally ordered that these crewmen be given a friendly reception.

Thus the crews would be staying in the dormitory constructed for them for several weeks or even months. This meant that Tomari village locals would be in and out of the dormitory, meeting the crewmen. They would learn Karate techniques from any military men who might be among them, which led to the unique features of Tomari style Kenpo.

---

[4] Hyochaku 漂着 to drift ashore or become shipwrecked. This seems to be talking about ships (that may or may not have been trade ships) that arrived damaged and had to be repaired.

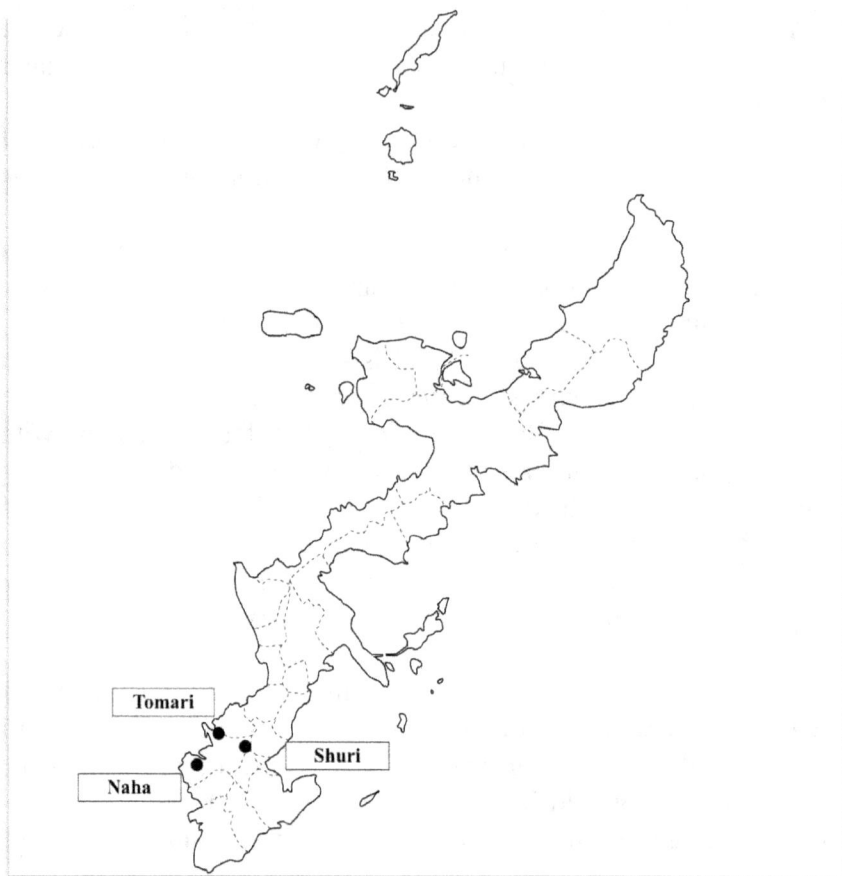

Map of Okinawa Main Island by the translator

Unfortunately, later on people developed their own explanation for how Tomari style came about without understanding the above explanation. They mistakenly proclaim that this is a Chinese style of martial arts being promulgated in Ryukyu. Moreover, they claim the basic postures have been fundamentally altered from the original. However the fundamental posture has always been with the feet in Hachimonji, facing outward like the Kanji Hachi 八, or eight. The way power is transmitted and the way the feet are used are uniform. There are no substantial differences between them. There are some advantages and disadvantages to each style. However, in the end, for people that train, the focus is always the focus always returns to being nimble. To having nimble movement, which is fundamental.

唐手の種類と變遷

唐手の種類は、餘りに多く、中には忘れられたるもあり、又は現在行はれざるもあつて、その消長發達も實に複雑で、世の變遷と共に唐手にも、よく流行せる型と、流行らない型の二種があり、從つて琉球に於ける分布狀態も自から異れるかの感がある。先づ古來より、琉球に行はれたるは、サンチン、五十四步、セーサン、セーユンチン、一百零八、ナイハンチ（三段）、パツサイ（大・小）チントー、チンテー、ワンシュー、ローハイ、及び公相君で、尤も廣く一般に行はれたるは、ナイハンチ、パツサイ、公相君の三種であつた。

而も、琉球の拳法卽ち唐手は、古來より支那から傳來し來たれるものであるが、サンチン、五十四步、セーサン、セーユンチン、一百零八は、支那でもよく流行り、現在なほ存在せるも、ナイハンチ、パツサイ、チントー、チンテー、ワンシュー、ローハイ及び公相君は、今や本存の支那では見ることさへ出來ず、只沖繩においてのみ、流行つてゐるのである。尙ほ、廢藩前までは、ワンシュー、ローハイの二種は泊のみで行はれ、首里・那覇では、之を稽古する人もなく、廢藩後に至つて、首里・那覇でもよくこれを敎へることゝなつたもの〳〵如く、平安に至りては、近世の武人糸洲先生がその子弟の敎材に資せんため、創案せられたもので、實に沖繩獨特の拳法で斯界のため大ひに喜ばしき次第である。

Types of Karate and their Vicissitudes

There are innumerable types of Karate, some of which have been forgotten. Some of these types of Karate are simply no longer practiced, and the story of how some developed and prospered and then decayed is quite complex. The vicissitudes of world events. affected Karate and this resulted in two types of Kata: Kata that became popular and Kata that were not popular.

Thus you can sense how these Kata are distributed differently throughout Ryukyu.

First of all, from days long past the following Kata have been practiced in Ryukyu:

Sanchin, Gojushi Ho, Se-san, Se-yunchin, Suparinpei, Naihanchi (Sandan, Third Level) Passai (Dai / Sho, Big and Small) Chintoo, Chintee, Wanshuu, Ro-hai as well as Kusanku.

The most generally practiced are the following three: Kusanku, Naihanchi, Passai and Kusanku.

However Ryukyu Kenpo, commonly referred to as Karate, Chinese Hand, was originally transmitted from China. The techniques Sanchin, Gojushi Ho, Se-san, Se-yunchin and Suparinpei are popular and China and you can still find people practicing them there. However, Naihanchi, Bassai, Chintoe, Chintee, Wanshuu and Robai as well as Kusanku you cannot find anyone who has even seen these techniques in China today. At the same time, it is quite popular to practice these techniques in Okinawa.

Before the Meiji government began the process of replacing the hundreds of feudal Domains with a smaller number of Prefectures in 1871, Wanshuu and Ro-hai were only practiced in Tomari, while no one trained these techniques in Shuri or Naha. Following the switch from Domains to Prefectures, these techniques began to be practiced extensively in Shuri and Naha.

As far as Pinan goes, the martial artist who only passed away recently, Itosu Sensei, developed it as a teaching method for his students. This is actually a Kenpo technique original to Okinawa and it has been well received in the Karate community.

拳法小則

（イ）唐手の稽古……十二歳を初期として、稽古を初むれば、いちぢるしく發達をなし、且つ、組織的にもよく訓練さるゝ便宜がある。しかしやる氣さへあれば何時から初めても出來る。なるべく、終身持續的に練習した方が、身體の爲めにも技の爲めにもよい。

（ロ）唐手の稽古に志し、又は研究中の者は、常に力の弱い方に力を盡し、稽古の時も、左手を多く役立たす様に心掛け、朝夕二回の稽古の時も、必ず出來る丈け左手の力を増進せしめる様に練習を積ねばならん。

（ハ）唐手の稽古をなし、且つ又武を練らんと欲する者は、常に起床の時も、床の上で坐り直つたまゝ、丹田にウンと力を入れ、兩三回左右の兩手を交互に平面或は前後左右に動かし、二本の手の發育に資するやうに力めねばならぬ。

（二）苟くも、唐手の修業をなす人は、其の基本姿勢八文字立を忘れない様に、稽古の時に限らず、出來得る丈け、胸を張り、下腹にウンと力を入れて、姿勢を正し、決して、その姿勢をくづさぬ様注意せねばならぬ。永く唐手の稽古をよくせる人は、普通の人より、何れも體格が立派で、頭健であるのは、常に稽古の時、胸を張り、力を丹田に入れ、而も姿勢をくづさぬ結果、それが習慣性となり、次第に身體が、打てば

A Few Principles Regarding Kenpo

a) You should begin Karate training around the age of eleven or twelve. If you do so you will develop remarkably quickly. Further, the systematic methodology makes it easy to adapt to training. That being said, anyone with the desire to learn Karate can begin at any age. If you train consistently over the course of your life the Waza, techniques will become embedded in your body.

b) For those that have already begun training in Karate, as well as those who are in the initial stages of training, but cannot generate a lot of power, my advice is to focus on training your left hand. During both morning and evening training do your best to give your left hand an intensive workout. Do this in order to develop better strength in that hand.

c) For those who have already started Karate training as well as those who seek to learn martial ways, you should maintain this daily routine. As soon as you awaken, sit upright on the floor. Place power in the spot below your navel known as Tanden with a *Un!* sound. Holding your arms level, sweep them back and forth three times so that they cross in front of you. Twist your body left, right, backwards and forwards. This will serve to lay a foundation for strengthening your arms.

d) Anyone who is even considering beginning Shugyo, or intensive training, in Karate should not forget the *Kihon-Shisei Hachimonji*, fundamental stance of positioning your legs with your feet facing outward like the Kanji *Hachi* 八 eight. Even when not training, it is essential remember to keep your chest pressed outward and to focus your power in your lower abdomen with a sound of *Un!* Ensure that you do not allow yourself to slouch out of this stance. It is a well-known fact that people who train Karate have a greater level of strength and endurance than those that do not. This is because throughout training they keep the chest out and put power in Tanden 丹田, the center of your body, located below the navel. If you were to strike the body of a person who has made this a fundamental aspect of their training, the impact would make a ringing sound. This is not something that should be ignored.

鳴る様に鍛へ上げられて、頑丈さを增して來たわけで、決しておろそかにすべきでない。

（ホ）唐手修業者にして、往々稽古場の狹隘を論ずる者があるが、不心得も甚だしい、苟くも、武といふ精神さへある人なら、毎日朝夕二回、たとひ一間角の桝の中でも、如何やうにも稽古は出來るから、缺かさず修練するやう心掛けねばならない。亦腹習といふ意味に於ても、練習者の必須條件であるから、常習的に試みるがよい。

（ヘ）唐手の修業者が、血氣に逸り、或は身を護らず、之を亂用して弱者いぢめをしては、不心得も甚だしい。修業者は常に武といふ一字を體して、謙讓克己の精神で、終始武の觀念を寸時も忘れてはならぬ。

（ト）唐手は、精神修養の一資料としても、實に有意義な世界的武術で、唐手を稽古した人は、精神の統一、鍛練が恐ろしい程發達して、物事に動ぜず、自から沈着になる、此處等は禪學と相一致する所が有る。

e) Frequently you will hear a person training in Karate complain about the strict instruction at the Dojo. However, such people do not have a true understanding of what training is about. A person with an understanding of the spirit of the Kanji *Bu* 武 martial arts and warrior, will conduct training twice a day once in the morning, once in the evening. You can easily conduct training in a square room with the sides only one *Ken* 間 1.8 square meters/ 5.9 square feet. It is important to maintain a regimen of training. Further it is important to do this training as a method of *Fukushu* 復習 review, which is an important aspect for practitioners to remember. This is a good goal to set for your customary training.

f) There are those that worry people doing intensive training in Karate are volatile or that they are not training Karate for self-defense, but instead intend to use it to bully and terrorize those who are not as strong. To those who are worried or anxious, let me allay your fears. Karate practitioners try to mold themselves into the Kanji *Bu* 武 which means both martial arts and warrior. By exercising self-control and maintaining modesty they seek to continually re-enforce in themselves the concept that they are martial artists and warriors.

g) Karate is a practical method of developing both your physical and mental strength. In fact, this valuable martial art can be done by anyone, anywhere in the world. If you practice Karate you will be able to unify your mind, eliminating the gap between thought and action. The training that forges the body will lead to an almost fearful development in your body. You be able to remain calm in any situation and control your reaction to anyone. These features of Karate are similar to the study of Zen meditation.

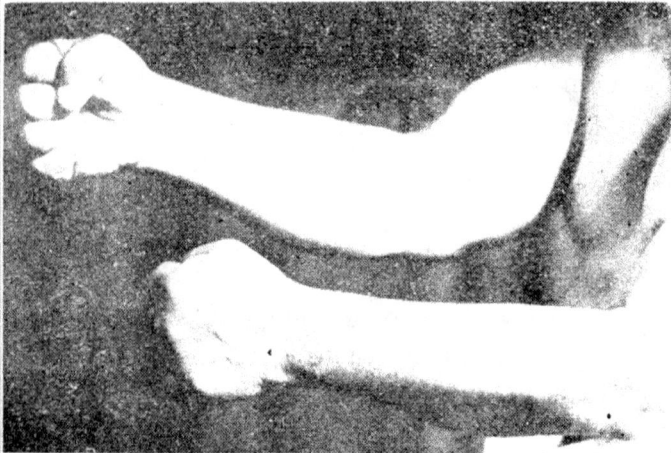

拳骨（テージクン）の握り方

琉球の拳骨は、昔から唐手の基本姿勢が、八文字立と決まってる様に、拳骨の握り方も亦一定してゐる。先づ握る順序を申せば、

最初に四本の指（人差指・中指・無名指・小指）を真すぐ延べ、指先より次第に蠻む如く深く握ると共に、拇指を曲げて、人差指中指間指の上に横たはる様に力を入れておくのである。

上図は、握りたる拳骨の表裏を示したものである。

Teejikun no Nigiri Kata
How to Make a Fist That Best Utilizes the Bones of the Hand

In the Ryukyu islands a fist is called Kenkotsu. The word Kenkotsu consists of two Kanji, *Ken* 拳 meaning fist and *Kotsu* 骨 meaning bone. In Japanese this is pronounced *Kenkotsu* while in the Ryukyu language this is pronounced *Teejikun*.

The Kihon Shisei, or basic positioning, that has existed since long ago was standing with your feet in Hachimonji, angled outward like the bottom of the Kanji Hachi 八 eight, with your fists gripped in Teejikun. A description of how to make this fist is as follows:

Extend the first four fingers of your hand,
(Hitosashi Yubi 人差指 "pointing at people finger" or index finger・Naka Yubi 中指 middle finger・Mumei Yubi 無名指 "nameless finger" or ring finger・Ko Yubi 小指 little finger)

Starting from the fingertips, gradually curl your fingers towards your palms as if you are folding them up deep in inside. At the same time bend your Oya Yubi 親指 "parent finger" or thumb, so that it is across your Hitosashi Yubi and Naka Yubi, index and middle fingers. From there put power in your fists.

The illustration on the previous page shows the Kenkotsu, or Teejikun, fist from both the outside and the inside.

Translator's Note:

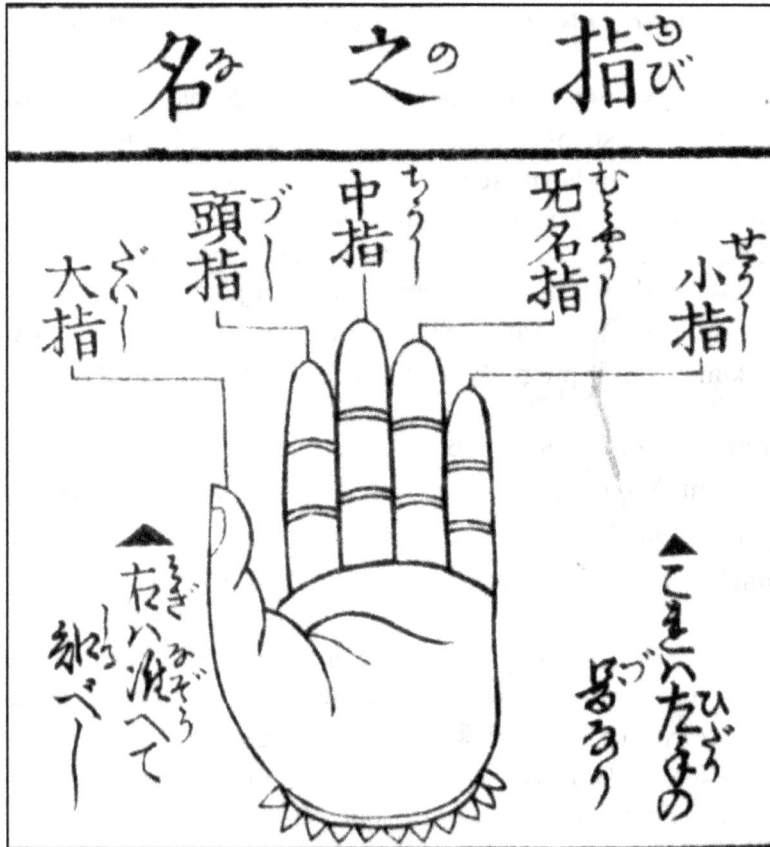

Chart showing the names of the fingers
From : Kuji Goshin Ho 九字護身法
Kuji for Self-Defense 1881

Translator's Note:

Names of the Fingers

Zushi   Chushi   Mushoshi
(Hitosashi Yubi) (Naka Yubi)   (Kusuri Yubi)

Daishi   Shoshi
(Oyayubi)   (Koyubi)

Understand that the names are the same for the right hand

This an the illustration of the left hand

Each finger has two names and multiple ways of writing them. In this illustration, the name on top is the old name for the finger and the one underneath in brackets is the contemporary Japanese name. This illustration is from *Kuji Goshin Ho* 九字護身法 *Kuji for Self-Defense* was written in 1812 by a Buddhist priest known only as Gyochi. It was published in 1881.

夫婦手の型

實戰の場合には、兩手は常に前圍の如く、くつ付けて置かねばならぬ。普通夫婦手と稱して居る。この兩手を如何運用するかと言へば、前の手は前線に立って戰ふので、攻撃もすれば防禦もする、即ち突く或は敵の攻撃を受けはづすと同時に、直ぐ突くので、後の手は常に豫備として置くので、前の手で間に合ぬ時に、後の手を以て攻撃もすれば、防禦もするのである。この構へ方は、普通知らないやうだ。よく構へるのに、片手丈け前方に突き出し、片手を脇腹に付けて、突く用意をなし、前の手を防禦即ち死手、後の手を攻撃即ち生手と稱して居る方もあるが、實際に適合しない考へ方で、誤れるも甚だしいのである。

斯様な構へ方では、實戰の場合に手後れとなるおそれがある。攻撃する手は、なるべく敵に近いのが有利で、結極敏活なる活動が出來るのである。この構へ方が、組手に應用せらるゝのを見たら、其効果の偉大なる事を悟られるであらう。

Mefutote no Kata
Husband and Wife Hands Kata[5]

In a Jissen, real combat, situation, both hands should be positioned as shown in the picture on the previous page. This stance is usually called *Mefutote* the Husband and Wife Hands. As for the question of how this stance is used the answer is your front hand is the one on the battle line doing the fighting. With that hand you can either launch an attack or use it to defend. In other words, that hand is used to punch or knock your opponent's attack aside and then immediately drive in with your own strike. The back hand is referred to as Yobi, being in a state of readiness. If the timing of your front hand is off, you can use your rear hand to attack or defend. This Kamae does not seem to be widely known.

I frequently see people standing with one hand forward and the other hand pulled back to Waki Bara, by the side under the armpit, ready to strike. This front hand is used only for defense. In other words it is what is known as a *Shi-te*, dead hand. The back hand is for attack and is therefore known as the *Iki-te,* living hand. This is not a logical way to position yourself for a real fight and the stance is riddled with mistakes.

Holding your hands in this position means that in a real battle your response will be delayed. It is most advantageous to have the hand you are attacking with close to your opponent, which makes the best use of quick and nimble style of fighting. Once you have seen this style of Kamae in Kumite you will realize how impressively effective it is.

---

[5] Motobu Choki writes it as Mefutode (due to old Kana usage this would probably have been read as Meutode,) however it is generally written as Meotode these days.

壹本拳（コーサー）の握り方

琉球では、昔から一本拳の握り方も、不言不語の中に習慣性となつて、一定の法則に依りて、子供時代からよく寫眞に示すが如き、握り方で一本拳を握つてゐる。

先づ最初に、中指無名指小指の三本を同時に曲げ、次に人差指を一層高く出し、指頭の横を拇指で壓へて、特に、拇指と人差指に力を入れるのである。尤も、一本拳の時人差指を使ふも中指を使ふも任意であるが、自分の寶驗からすると、次圖の握り方で、人差指と中指の二酏で當るやうに突いた方が効果がよいやうに思ふ。

Ippon Ken (Koosaa) no Nigiri Kata
How to Form One Finger Fist

From days long past in Ryukyu the method for making Ippon Ken, One Finger Fist, has been transmitted without words or language. Despite this, it has become a traditional method with its own rules. This method of gripping called Ippon Ken is shown in the picture on the following page and trained by practitioners starting from when they are children.

First of all bend your Naka Yubi, Mumei Shi (Yubi) and Ko Yubi, middle, ring and little fingers at the same time. Next, bend your Hitosashi Yubi, index finger, so it extends forward beyond the other three fingers and press down on the side of the end of that finger with your Oya Yubi, thumb.

In particular, put power in your Oya Yubi and Hitosashi Yubi. Typically Ippon Ken uses the Hitosashi Yubi, however it can be done with the Naka Yubi as well. Considering my own training with this method of striking, in my opinion, striking with the knuckles of both the Hitosashi Yubi and the Naka Yubi extended is the most effective. This is shown in the following picture.

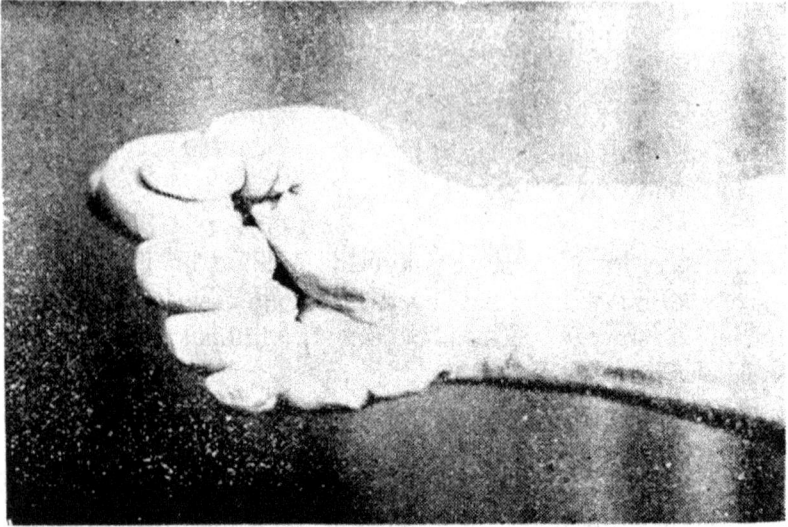

上圖は一拳未の握り方を示す

Illustration showing how to make *Ikkenpon* 一拳本 one-knuckle fist.

Translator's Note:
Kenpo Jutsu From *Various Tales from the Southern Isles*

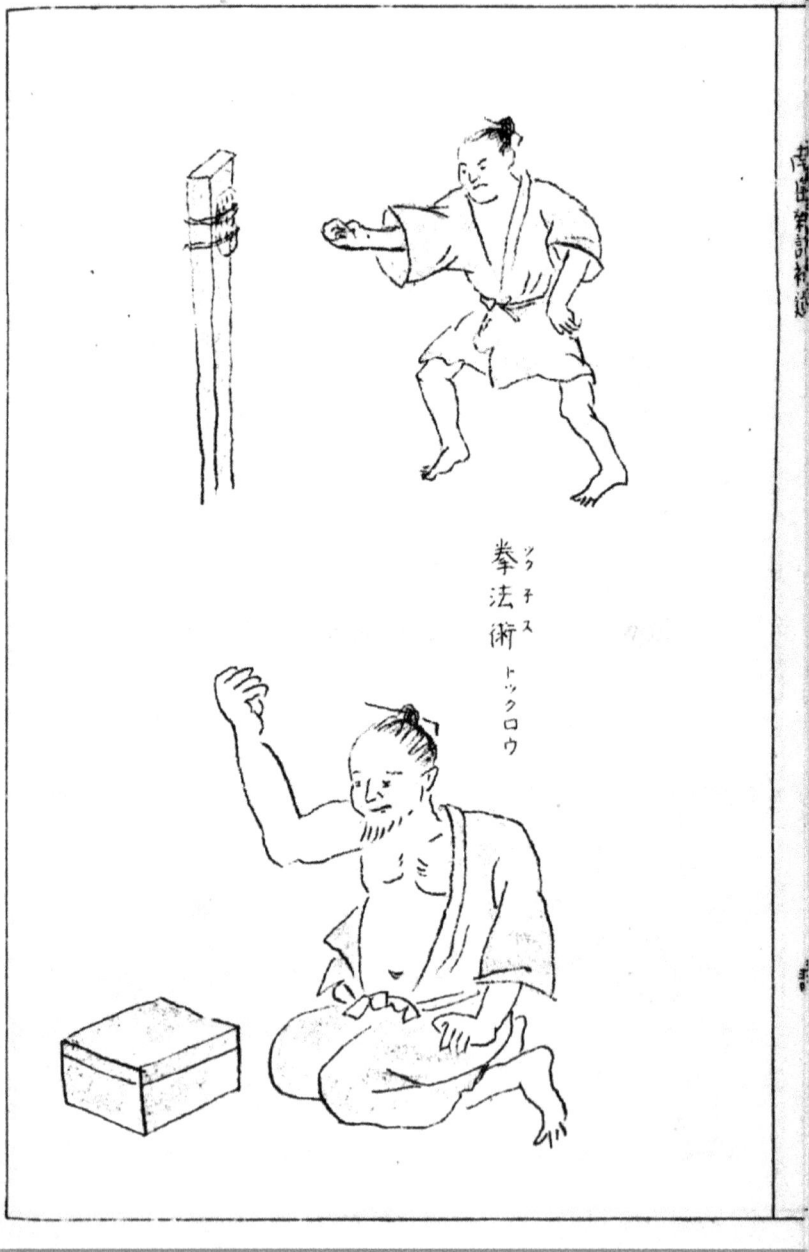

Translator's Note:
Kenpo Jutsu From *Various Tales from the Southern Isles*

The illustration on the previous page showing striking practice is from the book *Nanto Zatsuwa* 南島雑話 *Various Tales from the Southern Isles*. "The Southern Isles" was a common way to refer to the Ryukyu islands in Japan before the name Okinawa became common. The book contains an illustration of how men trained with Makiwara and some sort of wooden or stone box.

The inscription reads:

拳法術 *Kenpo Jutsu* – Way of the Fist Techniques
つく子ス *Tsukunesu* – Kneading the Hand. This is the way the word "Kenpo Jutsu" was read in the Amami islands.
トツクロウ *Totsu Kurou*– Totsu might be the word Totsu 突 to strike and Kuro might refer to drumming as in *Kurou* 鼓楼 the Chinese style towers that held signal drums.

This book was written and illustrated beginning in 1850 by a man named Nagoya Sagen. He was part of an unsuccessful plot to overthrow the succession of a noble house. This was known as *O-Ie Sodo* 御家騒動, "house strife."

While most of the other conspirators were made to commit seppuku, Nagoya Sagen was banished to Amami Oshima Island in March of 1850. While in exile he studied the island and its local customs and recorded his observations along with illustrations.

基本姿勢と腰

唐手の練習上、常に心掛くべきは、其の基本姿勢と力の入れ方即ち腰の据ゑ方である。

基本姿勢は、前述の通り、何れの場合と雖も八文字立で、八字形に爪先を開き、足と足との間隔は、人に依つて多少の差異はあるが、大凡一尺五寸位を基準としたらよからう、亦力の入れ方も、兎に角腰を据ゑて、下腹にウンと力を入れる様に、常に心掛けねばならぬ。この型は、人間が歩む時の自然の形ちからきたもので、姿勢の突方及びナイハンチ第三図の立方も、この八文字型である。

Kihon Shisei to Koshi
Basic Posture and the Hips

One thing you should always pay attention to when training Karate is the Kihon Shisei, Basic Stance, and Chikara no Irikata, how and where to focus your power. This is referring to how to position your hips.

The Kihon Shisei is as described before, you will always have your feet in Hachimonji, shaped like the Kanji Hachi 八 eight. The toes of your feet should be pointed outwards like the bottom of the Kanji Hachi 八 eight. However, this distance can be different from person to person however, 1 Shaku 5 Sun, 45.5 centimeters/ 18 inches, is the standard distance.

With regards to where to put power, the most important thing is to always remember to lower your hips, focus your power in your lower abdomen with a shout of *Un!* This method was developed from the natural way that humans walk. The Tsuki Kata, way of striking, as well as the stance shown in the third picture of Naihannchi also contain this Hachimonji stance.

卷藁の作り方と其の稽古法

唐手修業者の必備品の中に、卷藁といふ稽古用具がある。拳骨の鍛錬に資するもので、これによつて数ヶ月鍛へられたら、拳はよく数枚の瓦や板を、一撃の下に粉碎することが出來る。

卷藁には、提卷藁と立卷藁の二通りあるが、普通、立卷藁のことを戦に「マキワラ」と稱し、使用者も多いが、提卷藁は立卷藁のやうに常に使用されず、且つ使用する人も少いのである。

今其の作り方を詳述せば、

提卷藁は十束位の藁の中に五十斤程の砂を入れ、長さ一尺五寸の四尺廻りにして、更に繩で固く卷きつけ、それを兩端より提繩を掛け、上に吊るして突くやうになつてゐる。

立卷藁は、藁で平紐を作り、わらに卷きつけ、長さ一尺幅三寸五分程の所謂「マキワラ」をこさえ、これを卷

一一

How to Make a Makiwara and How to Use it for Training

One piece of equipment essential to the development of your Karate technique is the Makiwara, or tied bundle of rice straw. It is excellent for forging Kenkotsu, your fists. After just a few months of training with this you can easily smash through several boards or roof tiles with a single punch.

There are two varieties of Makiwara, the *Sage Makiwara* 提巻藁 Suspended Straw Bale, and the Ritsu Makiwara, Standing Straw Covered Striking Board. For the most part, practitioners use the Ritsu Makiwara so it is generally referred to simply as Makiwara. The use of the Sage Makiwara, "Suspended Straw Bale" is not as common as the Ritsu Makiwara, "Standing Straw Covered Striking Board" and, truth be told, not many people use it. Next, I would like to describe how these are made.

Sage Makiwara : Hanging Straw Target Bale

First of all, to make the Sage Makiwara 提巻藁 Hanging Straw Target Bale, roll up ten rolls of rice straw with fifteen Kin of sand inside (One Kin 斤 = 0.6 kilograms/ 1.3 pounds. 15 Kin= 9 kilograms/20 pounds.)

Your Hanging Straw Target Bale should be 1 Shaku 5 Sun, 45 cm/ 18 inches tall and 120 cm/ 48 inches around. Next, wrap it firmly with rope. Finally, attach a piece of rope to each end, hang it up and use it for striking.

Translator's Note: Illustrations of Makiwara

空手道入門 *An Introduction to Karatedo* Mabuni Kenwa 1938 *Sage Makiwara* Hanging Bale of Rice Straw	図解空手入門 *An Illustrated Introduction to Karate* Konishi Yasuhiro 1953 *Tsurushi Tawara* Hanging Bale (a type of Makiwara)
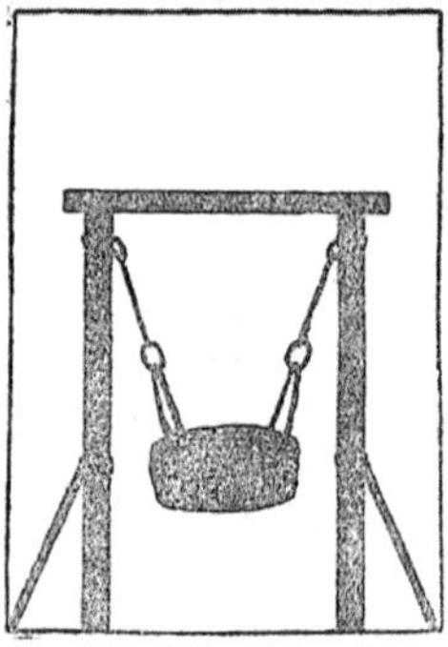 第三〇圖 下げ卷藁	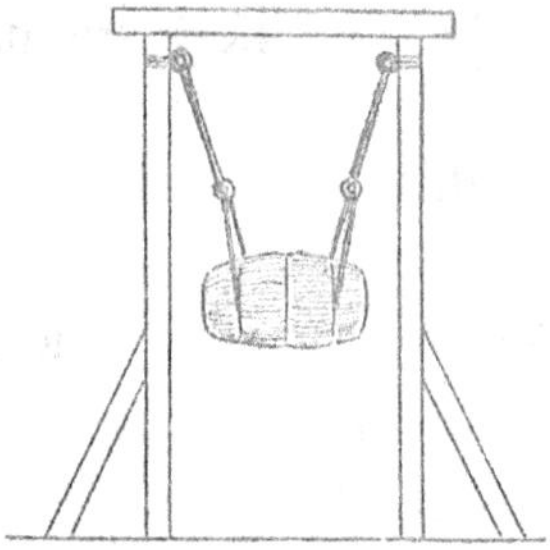 吊し俵（卷藁の一種）

Translator's Note: Illustrations of Makiwara

空手道入門 : 図解説明 Introduction to Karate: An Illustrated Guide 1951 Ooya Reikichi	
This is a sack filled with sand or sawdust used to train the hips. Hang it at about chest level.	*This is for toughening the hands and feet. It is the same as the Makiwari used in Kyudo, Japanese Archery.*
	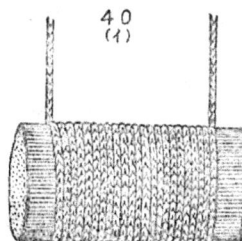

Translator's Note: Illustrations of Tachi Makiwara

Introduction to Karate: An Illustrated Guide
Ooya Reikichi 1951

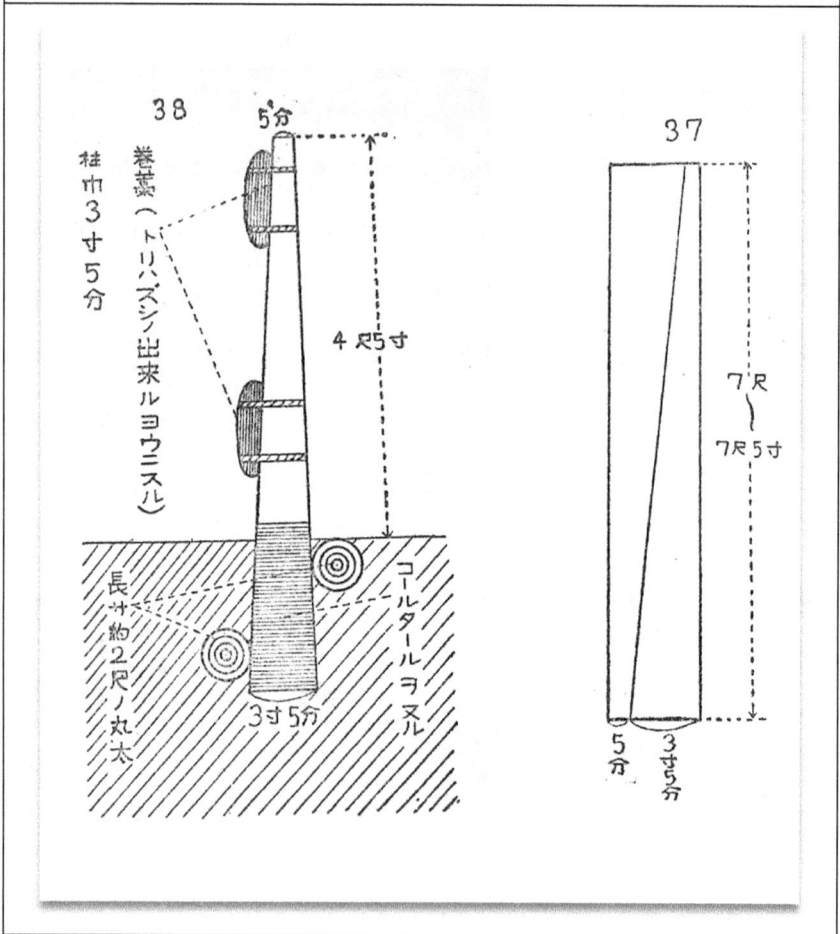

Translator's Note: Illustrations of Tachi Makiwara

Introduction to Karate: An Illustrated Guide
Ooya Reikichi 1951

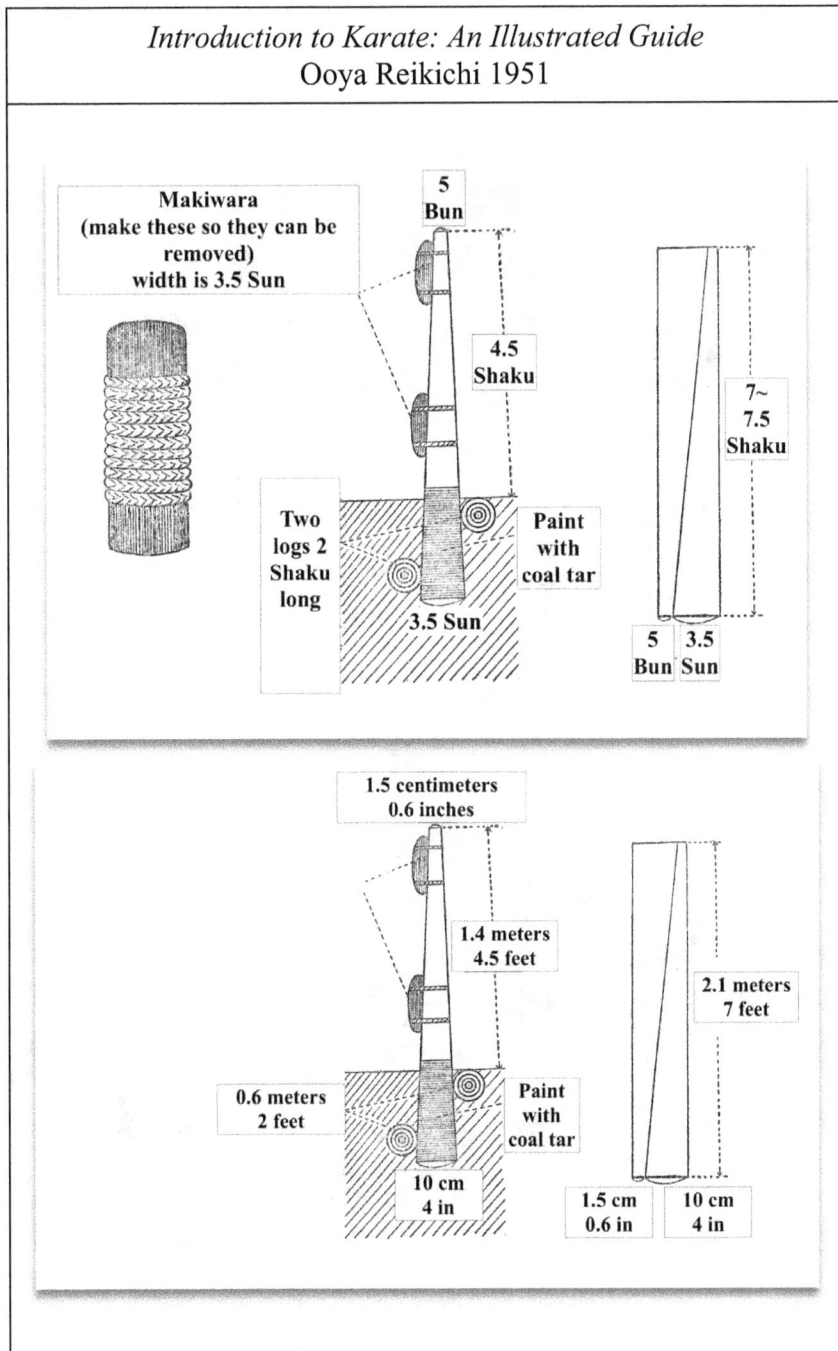

Makiwara
(make these so they can be removed)
width is 3.5 Sun

5 Bun

4.5 Shaku

7~ 7.5 Shaku

Two logs 2 Shaku long

Paint with coal tar

3.5 Sun

5 Bun   3.5 Sun

1.5 centimeters
0.6 inches

1.4 meters
4.5 feet

2.1 meters
7 feet

0.6 meters
2 feet

Paint with coal tar

10 cm
4 in

1.5 cm
0.6 in

10 cm
4 in

Translator's Note: Illustrations of Tachi Makiwara

Introduction to Karate: An Illustrated Guide (1951)
Ooya Reikichi

次に卷藁の作り方ですが、卷藁は第三九圖のようなもので、藁を束ねて長さ一尺二寸位・幅三寸五分位・厚さ二・三寸位の大きさにして、藁縄でしつかりと卷きます。この藁縄は、しつかりと三ツ組みによつたものが、なければ普通の藁縄でもよろしい。卷き終ると槌か棒で叩いて、少し平らたくしておきます。尚この卷藁の代りに布を重ねて使用しても結構です。

Translator's Note: Illustrations of Tachi Makiwara

Introduction to Karate: An Illustrated Guide (1951)
Ooya Reikichi

Next, regarding making Makiwara. The Makiwara should be made as shown in illustration 39 on the previous page. Make a bundle of Wara, rice straw about 1 Shaku 2 Sun long, 36.3 cm/ 14 in, and about 3 Sun 5 Bun wide, 10.6 cm/ 4 in, and 2 or 3 Sun thick, 6~9 cm/ 2.4~3.6 in.

Use rice straw rope to bind the bunch securely. I recommend that you use rice-straw rope that has been securely braided. If such rope is not available, then simple rice-straw rope is fine. After you finish tying, strike it with a wooden mallet or stick in order to flatten it out. It is also acceptable to use a folded piece of cloth in place of rice straw

藥木にくびり付けて、突くのであるが其の大きさは、普通左の通りになってゐる。

巻藥木は……一、全長　七　尺（地上四尺五寸地下二尺五寸）

一、幅　　三寸五分（後圖の如し）

一、厚さ　上端　五分　　下端　二寸五分

又立巻藥の一種で、重に兩腕の發育に資するマキワラといふ、稽古用具もあり、餘り一般には用ひられないが、特に、參考の爲に詳述しておく。この巻藥は、巻藥木を圓くして、直徑三寸程の長さ七尺のものを地上四尺五寸、地下二尺五寸の割にて、地中に動かぬやうに埋め、厚さ一寸以上にして長さ一尺位のマキワラで固く巻きつけて、兩腕を正面或は側面より打ちかけ、筋骨の發達に資する様になってゐる。

尚ほ、巻藥の突き方は、胸を出來るだけ張り、八文字形に立ち、左右の兩手を以て交互に突く、第一圖（左手）第二圖（右手）足も亦第三圖の如く、最初右足を突出して練習をやり、次に第二圖の如く、左足を突出して前同様練習を繰返す。

茲に注意すべきは、巻藥の稽古の時、突の手が八分の力でいく時は、引く力は十分の力を必ず出して、稽古す

一二

Tachi Makiwara #1: Standing Straw Covered Striking Board

The Tachi Makiwara is made with parallel wrappings of rice straw cord. This straw cord is wrapped firmly around a flat board and when finished is about 1 Shaku 30 centimeters/ 12 inches long and about 3 Sun 5 Bun 10 cm/ 3.6 inches wide. The dimensions are as follows:

- The total height is 7 Shaku, 210 centimeters/ 7 feet.
  2.5 Shaku, or 75 cm/ 2'6", should be buried underground
  4.5 Shaku, or 135 cm/ 4'4", above ground
- Width 3 Sun, 10 cm/ 3.6 inches
- It should be 5 Bun, 1.5 cm/ 0.6 inches thickness at the top and 2 Sun 5 Bun 7.6 cm / 3 inches thick at the bottom.

There is actually a second kind of Tachi Makiwara that is used to strengthen and develop the arms. This is called simply Makiwara and it is not commonly used but I thought I would include a description of it here.

Tachi Makiwara #2 : Standing Straw Covered Striking Pole

This type of Makiwara uses the type of wood as the previous striking board, but rounded. It is 9 cm/ 3.6 inches in diameter. The total height is 7 Shaku, 210 cm/ 7 feet, but 2.5 Shaku, or 75 cm/ 2.5 feet, should be buried firmly in the ground so that it does not move. The remaining 4.5 Shaku, or 135 cm/ 4 feet, is above ground. Pieces of Wara, rice grass straw rope, at least 3 cm/1.2 inches thick and about 30 cm/12 inches long should be wrapped and tied firmly to the pole which can them be used to train the arms either by striking it straight on or from this side. This will help to develop the muscles and bones in the arms.

べきで、左の手から始めねばならぬ。何となれば、何れの人にしても、左は右より力量において、常に劣つて居るもので、右が二十突く時は、左は三十回、右が三十回つく時は、左は四十回といふ調子で朝夕缺かさず、稽古する様心掛けねばならぬと思ふ。

亦第四圖の如く、卷藥の横に立ち、手の側面を以て打ち練習す（右左共同様なり）。

亦第五圖の如く、足の稽古をなす卽ち土踏まずと足指との中間を以て蹴るのである。

提卷藥は主に足の稽古をなすに用ひ、踵及土踏まずと足指との中間指先の三方の練習をなす事を忘れてはならぬ。

尤も、提卷藥は、作り方が上下に自由に動く様になつて居るから、昔から足や手或は臂裏をもつて、便宜突いたり、又は打ちかけて、筋骨の發育にも資したものである。

一三

Training Makiwara

1   2   3

It is important to remember that when practicing striking the Makiwara you should be standing in Hachimonji with your chest out and alternate striking with your left and right hands. This is shown in Picture 1 (the left hand) and Picture 2 (the right hand.)

As for your feet, as Pictures 1 and 2 show, you begin with your right foot forward. Then, as shown in Picture 3, train in the same way but with your left foot forward.

The thing I would like you to be most careful of when doing Makiwara training is that when putting 80% power into your punch ensure that you pull that strike back with 100% power. Please train in this manner.

When training it is logical to begin with your left hand. Many people tend to be right handed and therefore their left hand has less power. You can correct this balance when training by doing thirty strikes with the left for every twenty with the right. Similarly, if you do thirty strikes with your right hand then do forty with your left. You should make it a goal to do this type of training consistently twice a day, once in the morning and once in the evening.

4   5

Picture 4 shows how you stand to the side of the Makiwara and practice striking with the side of your hand (you should train both your left and right hands.)

Picture 5 shows how you train your feet. Specifically you are kicking with the space between your *Tsuchi Fumazu* 土踏まず "Doesn't Touch the Ground" or the arch of your foot, and your toes.

The main purpose of the Sage Makiwara is to train the feet by kicking in the following three ways:

- Kicking with the heel
- Kicking with the spot between the toes and the arch of the foot
- Kicks with the ends of the toes

It is important not to forget this.

The construction of the Sage Makiwara allows you to raise or lower it as you need. Throughout the history of Karate the Sage Makiwara, Hanging Straw Bale, has been used as convenient way strengthen the bones and muscles of the hands, feet and elbows. You can also practice striking it, which serves to develop the muscles and bones.

Translator's Note: Illustrations of Kicks By Mabuni Kenwa

空手道入門
An Introduction to Karatedo
Mabuni Kenwa
1938

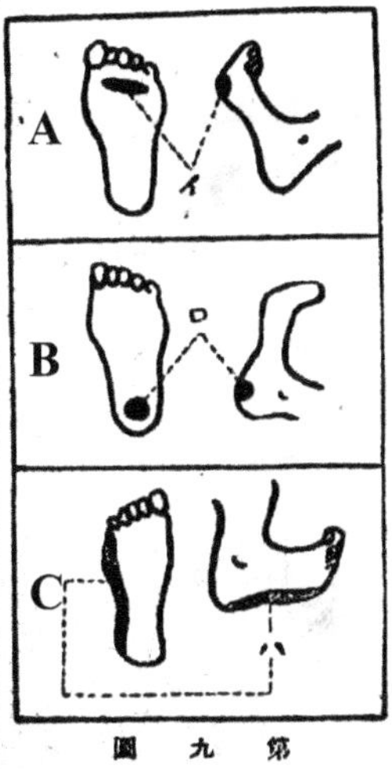

をなし、又下方へ強く踏み下ろして敵の足の甲を踏みくだく時等に用ふ。

▲足刀（第九圖ハ）足の小指側の側面を手刀と對應して足刀と名づけます。主として敵の膝關節を蹴る時に用ふ。

▲上足底（第九圖イ）足の裏面で足指の付け根の處を名づけます。蹴り上げる時に用ひます。

▲下足底（第九圖ロ）足の裏面で踵の部分を云ふ。蹴上げの時の補助的働き

第九圖

Jo-Sokutei – Upper Kick With the Bottom of the Foot. As shown in illustration A, kick using the Tsukene, where your toes meet the ball of the foot. Used when doing a Keri Age, Upward Kick.

Ka-Sokutei – Lower Kick With the Bottom of the Foot. As shown in illustration B, this refers to kicking with the Kakuto, heel. This part is used to assist a Keri Age, Upward Kick.

Soku Toh – Foot Katana. Using the side of your foot by your little toe to kick like a Shuto, knife hand. This is the origin of the name. Used primarily to kick the joint around your opponent's the knee.

Translator's Note: Illustrations of Kicks By Konishi Yasuhiro

---

図解空手入門
An Illustrated Introduction to Karate
Konishi Yasuhiro
1953

足の各部の名稱

第七圖イは上足底、ロは下足底（或は下踵）、ハは後踵（或はウシロカカト）、ニは足刀、ホは足首〉

イは敵の釣鐘（金的）其の他を蹴る時に用ひ、ロはイの蹴りの補助作用をなす外、敵の足を踏む時などにも用ふ。ハは矢印の如く後へ蹴りあげる。例へば敵が後から抱きついたとき、下踵で敵の足をドンと踏み、敵が其の足を引くと同時に後踵で金的へ蹴りあげることが出來る。足刀は横蹴りとして顛る偉力あるもの、足首は敵の股間に蹴り込んでその金的に打撃を與へる。圖には示してないが膝頭の蹴りも度々活用される。

前記イロハニの各部位の鍛錬は第二圖卷藁の柱の下部にとりつけた卷藁に當てゝ行ふ。蹴りは實戰の場合には「臍より高くを蹴るな」と古豪の戒めがあるが、平素は練習としては高く蹴ることも行はれて居る。然し遠くから大きく足を振る様に蹴るのではなく、後の足の踵を浮かさない程度で、立つたなゝの位置で高く蹴ることを練習する。

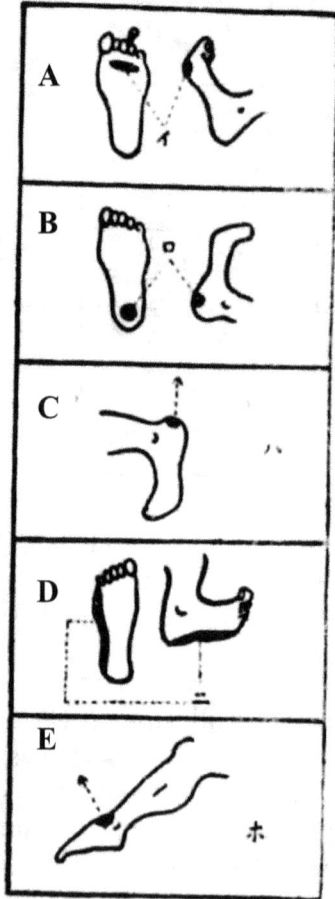

A イ
B ロ
C ハ
D ニ
E ホ

第七圖　足の各部

Translator's Note: Illustrations of Kicks By Konishi Yasuhiro

図解空手入門 *An Illustrated Introduction to Karate* (1953)

Names of Various Parts of the Foot
Illustration 7
A is *Jo-Sokutei* – Upper Kick With the Bottom of the Foot
B is *Ka-Sokutei* – Lower Kick With the Bottom of the Foot, also known as *Kasho*, Lower Heel.
C is *Kosho*, Back Heel, also known as *Ushiro Kakato*, Back Heel.
D is *Sokutoh*, Foot Katana.
E is *Ashi Kubi*, Ankle.

Point A is used to strike to strike to the groin. This vital point is known as Tsuri Gane, Hanging Bell, or Kinteki, Golden Target. It is also used when kicking to other places.

Point B is employed to assist when kicking with Point A and is also used to smash down on the top of an opponent's foot.

The arrow on **Point C** shows how to kick back and up with the heel. For example if an opponent wraps you up from behind, you can use your heel to smash down onto his foot and when he pulls that foot back use a back heel strike to kick upward into the groin.

Use the Foot Katana, **Point D**, as an extremely powerful side kick.

Use **Point E**, the ankle, to kick in between your opponent' legs to deliver a powerful blow to the groin. While not shown in the illustration above, the Hizagashira, Kneecap, can be used to kick in a multitude of situations.

To train the above mentioned kicks, A~E use the bottom part of a Makiwara pole.

There is a cautionary saying amongst old-timers that in a real fight, "Never kick a person above the navel," however kicking high is part of regular training. That being said this is not describing a big kick thrown from a distance. It is a kick where the heel of your back foot does not come off the ground. You are training how to kick high from a standing position.

一四

○巻藁の突方の説明

上の図の如く右足を突出し、八文字形に立ち、腰を据ゑ。

先づ左拳より始める。

最初、左拳を脇腹に図の如く臍へ、突き出すべし。

腕は途中より内側に捻じ、手の甲が上方に向く様にし、人差指中指の四節を以て突く、充分打ち伸すべし。

引く時には、充分力を入れて出來得る丈け、肘を後方に引くべし。

Makiwara no Tsuki-kata no Setsumei
How to Strike the Makiwara : Picture 1

As shown in the illustration, stand with your right foot forward with your feet in Hachimonji, shaped like the Kanji *Hachi* 八 eight, and your hips lowered.

Begin with your left hand.

First, begin with your left fist tucked in by your left side, then strike as shown in the picture.

Your fist should rotate inward as you are striking so that when you make contact with the Makiwara the back of your hand is facing up. Strike with the first two knuckles of your Hitosashi Yubi, index finger and Naka Yubi, middle finger. Be sure to extend your arm sufficiently even after making contact.

Pull your arm back quickly after striking, as if you are yanking your elbow backward.

但し突く時は八分、引く時は十分の力
を入れる。

總て前同様。

第二図右手の突方。

一五

Makiwara no Tsuki-kata no Setsumei
How to Strike the Makiwara : Picture 2

In other words, when striking, use 80% power and when pulling your arm back use 100% power.

Picture 2 shows how to strike with the right hand. This is done the same way as the left hand.

一六

第三圖左足を前方に突き出し、總て前同様。

但し、右利きの人は、左を右の二倍突くを可とす、猶は漸次熟練するに從ひ左右交互に突くやうに練習すべし。

Makiwara no Tsuki-kata no Setsumei
How to Strike the Makiwara : Picture 3

Picture 3 shows how to strike with the left foot forward. Other than that difference, the method is the same as described before.

However, right-handed people should train their left hand twice as much as their right hand. However, gradually, through diligent practice, you should aim for training by alternating your left and right hands.

四圖の如く、巻藁の側面に八文字形に
立ち、腰を据ゑ、拳の横面を以て突く
練習をなすべし。
是、か左右共練習するを忘れるべから
ず。

一七

Makiwara no Tsuki-kata no Setsumei
How to Strike the Makiwara : Picture 4

As picture 4 shows, while standing in Hachimonji beside the Makiwara, lower your hips and practice striking the side of the target.

Do not neglect to train both your right and left arms together.

五圖は足にて突く場合にして、充分打ち伸すべし。

一八

Makiwara no Tsuki-kata no Setsumei
How to Strike the Makiwara : Picture 5

Picture 5 shows how to strike with the feet. Ensure you extend your foot at the moment of contact.

練習器具

およそ、何れの運動に於ても、各其の性質に依りて形こそ異なれ、一定の練習用具がある如く、唐手の練習にも、亦缺く可からざる必要器具がある。然るに、その多くは、原始的時代よりそのまゝの練習器具で、文明の今日或は排斥する人もあらんも、此の原始的器具そここそ、唐手練習上缺くべからざる用具である。

先づ、初期の練習者に必要なものにして、力量の増進上、缺くべからざる物に、七十斤位の卵形の石がある。それは毎日朝夕二回練習者が肩にかたげて、自らの力の増進を計る必要品で、それより段々力が増すと共に百五十斤程度迄の卵形の石を使用する様心掛けねばならぬ。

猶は、両腕の力量を増進せしめるために使用するに、チーシー及びサーシーがある。

チーシーは、鬪鷄の石か鐵を以て製し、鎭中に一尺より一尺三寸位の木製の取り柄を差し込み其の柄の先を握りて、前後左右に差延べるのである。サーシーは錠前の形をなし、石で製したもので是れも矢張手の甲にの

せ、前後左右に差延べて両腕の力量増進の練習をするので、其の斤量は各人の腕力の如何に依りて異なるが、何れも大凡十斤程度である。

Renshu Kigu
Training Equipment

Every type of exercise uses training equipment in order to develop the body. Though the style of training may differ according to the nature of the exercise, each has its own type of training equipment. Karate also has essential training equipment. However, for the most part these training tools are primitive, having remained unchanged since long in the past. In these times of cultural enlightenment, many people are purging them. However, though they may be primitive, they are essential tools for improving your Karate training.

The first tool I would like to introduce is one that is essential for increasing your strength when you first begin training. It is an egg shaped stone that weighs about 70 Kin, 15 kilograms/ 93 pounds. Twice a day, morning and evening, you should lift this up on your shoulder. This is essential for increasing your strength. As you become stronger set a goal of increasing the weight of the egg shaped stone to one that is 130 Kin, 78 kilograms/ 172 pounds, in weight.

In addition, Chiishi and Saashii are used for building strength in the arms.

Chiishii are constructed out of rounded stone or iron. In the center, a 1 Shaku and 2 or 3 Sun, 36~39 cm/ 14~15 inch, length wooden handle is inserted. You train with Chiishii by holding the end of the handle and extending your arms out to the front, back, left and right.

Saashii are Jomae, lock shaped, weights carved out of stone. Train with these by holding them so the weight is on the backs of your hands and then extend your arms front, back, left and right.

This type of training will increase your arm strength. While the weight used will differ according to each person, generally speaking they should be about 10 Kin, 6 kilograms/ 13 pounds.

Translator's Note: Illustrations of *Chiishii* and *Saashii*

Training with Chiishii and Saashii

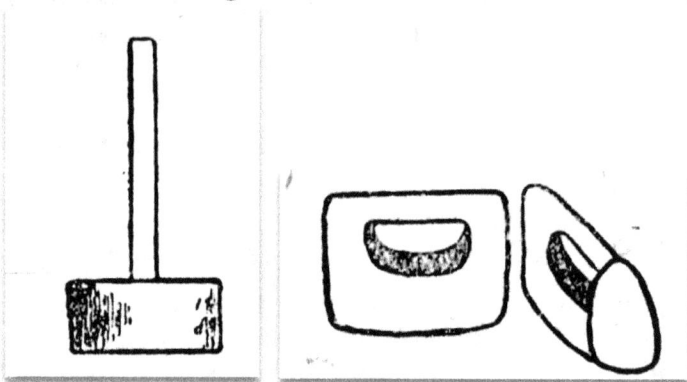

Chiishii and Saashii

Illustrations from: *An Introduction to Karatedo*
By Mabuni Kenwa 1938

Translator's Note: Chikara-Ishi

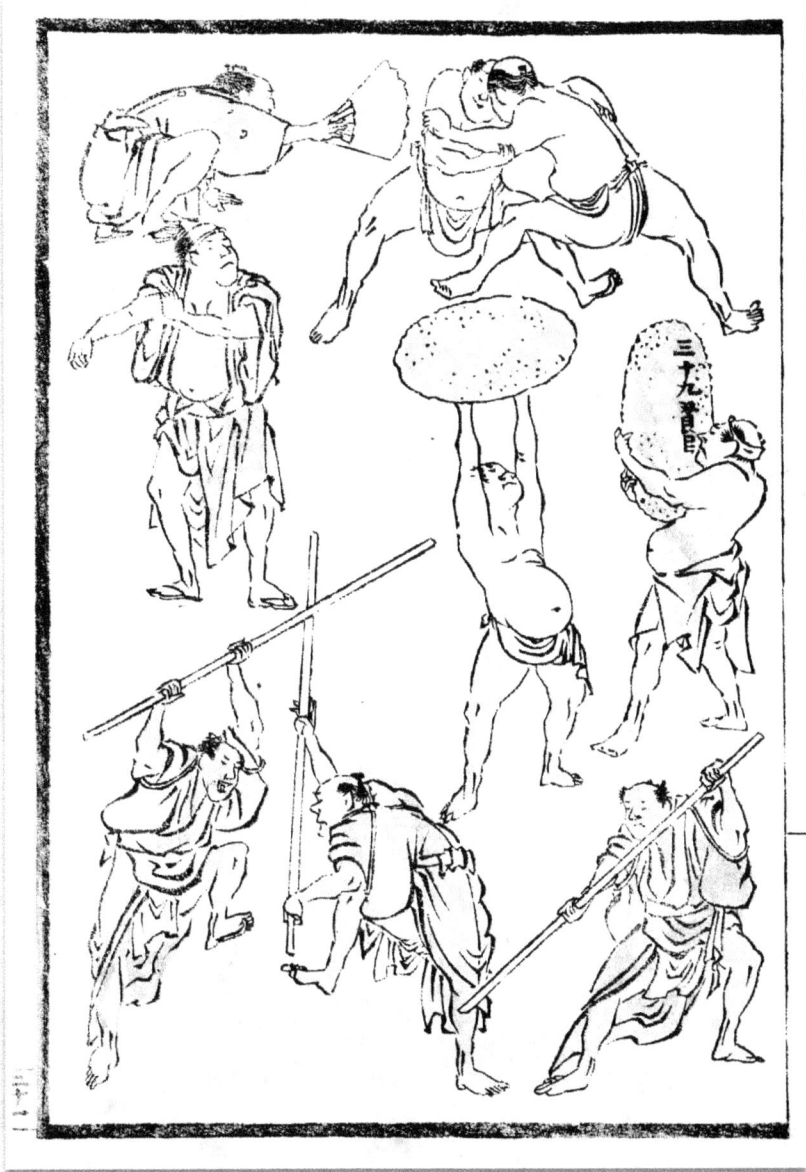

Sumo wrestlers training with Chikara-Ishi, Rocks of Strength. This rock has the weight carved into it: 39 Kan, 146 Kilograms / 321 pounds.

-From : 写真学筆 *A Study in Truthful Painting* 1815
-By Maki Bokusen (1736-1824)

稽古の心得（松村・長濱・糸洲翁の話）

俗に能く、力武士といふ言葉が有るが、昔から唐手を稽古するに、其の方法と心條が、師に依つて大分異る様である。此の事は、餘程肝要な事で、現在も心得違ひをして居る人々がある様で、殊に今後唐手を稽古する方々の爲めに、特に申上げて置きたいのである。那覇の長濱先生が、首里山川の松村先生をほめた話を例に引いて申上たい。

松村先生は、長濱先生よりは少し先輩であるが、中々ゆとりのある武柄で、決して力一方の武士ではなかつた。而して常に靜中動きを觀て運用自在であつた。私も久しく松村先生の許にはかよつて、教を受けたが、常に其の型の稽古は力の入れ方及び型の運用に意を注いで居れた。其れは樵に其の通りで、私も今日迄其の教へを遵奉して來て居る。たとへ力は他人に秀れ、身體は堅く鍛へてあつても、充分に其の技の運用を會得して居ないと、咄嗟の場合に、敏速なる活動が出來なくなるので、其の武は何等のやくにも立たなくなる。そこで糸洲先生はと

78

Keiko no Kokoroe
Lessons on Training from the Elderly Gentleman Matsumura, Nagahama & Itosu

Chikara Bushi is a colloquial term for a person who is a mighty warrior. Long ago, when training Karate, the method and mindset could vary a great deal depending on the teacher. This is an important element to consider especially since these days there are quite few people who misunderstand this and it will benefit those who will begin training Karate in the future. I would like to relate a complementary story about Matsumura Sensei of Shuri as told by Nagahama Sensei of Naha.

Matsumura Sensei is slightly senior to Nagahama Sensei. He was a martial artist who always seemed to have room to develop, rather than one who relied solely on strength. He was able to suddenly move from a state of complete stillness and had total freedom of movement. I went to Matsumura Sensei's dojo for instruction after a long absence and found his instruction focused on where to put power when doing Kata and how the movements should be done. I realized that clearly this is the way training should be conducted and have followed that method since then.

For example, if you have not learned the proper way to execute the movements, even if you are in better physical shape and are clearly stronger than your opponent, you will not be able to respond nimbly in an extreme situation. This means none of your martial arts techniques will be of any use.

普へば體格と言ひ、武力と言ひ、機に傑出した武人で寶兄が稽古する時には毎日の如に拙宅へ御出になつて居たので、私も十二三歳位の時から、一所に稽古した居たところが、私は何時も兄にいぢめられて居たので、どうしたら兄に勝つ事が出來るかと絶へず考へて居たので、遂ひに糸洲先生丈けでは、あきたらず、儀保の佐久間先生や松村先生の許に、ひそかに通ひ、種々と研究して、二十歳位からは機に兄に勝つ自信があつた。それでも糸洲先生の許へは、時々伺つて種々と批評を受けて居たが、先生が私を認める様になつてからの御話であつたが、長濱先生の遺言を打ちあけて話された事がある。

元來糸洲先生は、最初松村先生に教へを受けて居られたが、如何にも糸洲先生は鈍重で、先生の氣に入らなかつた。そこで熱心に稽古をするけれども、肝心の師の方でおろそかであつたので、遂ひに退つて那覇の長濱先生の許に通ふことになつた。長濱と糸洲は、一つちがいであつたが、師弟の關係を結んだのである。長濱先生は其の當時相當に名の賣れた方であつた。非常に熱心家で常に庭先で朝早くから、稽古を初め、夕日が大分西にかたむいて、稽古する影が妻君の機織にかゝる時を以て止められたそうである。

處が先生は松村先生とは反對に専ら力を出し、身體を堅める方に専念して、稽古をして居られたさうで、その

As for Itosu Sensei, whether you are talking about his physical body, or his martial ability, he was an outstanding martial artist. Itosu Sensei would visit my house nearly every day to teach me along with my older brother.[6] I was about twelve or thirteen years old at the time.[7] During training my older brother would always be rough with me. I thought continuously of ways to beat him and eventually realized I wouldn't be able to do this with Itosu Sensei's teachings alone, so I secretly began to attend lessons with Sakuma Sensei from Giho as well as Matsumura Sensei. I learned a great many things, and by the time I was twenty I was confident I could beat my brother. At the time I was also still attending lessons with Itosu Sensei and received valuable critiques and advice.

After Itosu Sensei had acknowledged that I had developed into a martial artist he granted me the honor of revealing the following anecdote about Nagahama Sensei.

The background of this story is that originally Itosu Sensei was a student of Matsumura Sensei. However as Itsou Sensei was quite a stubborn man, Matsumura Sensei took a dislike to him. Thus, despite the fact that Itosu Sensei was a diligent student, he was neglected by his teacher. This eventually led to Itosu Sensei withdrawing from that Dojo and beginning training under Nagahama Sensei in Naha. While Nagahama Sensei and Itosu Sensei were only a year apart in age, they had a firm master-student relationship. At the time Nagahama Sensei was quite well-known as a Karate instructor. He was a Karate practitioner completely devoted to his craft. Nagahama Sensei would begin training early in the morning in his garden and wouldn't stop until the sun was low in the west and his shadow had reached his wife's weaving loom.

However, Nagahama Sensei's training philosophy was the exact opposite of Matsumura Sensei's. His training focused exclusively on generating power and strengthening the body.

---

[6] Motobu Choyu 本部朝勇 (1865~1928)

[7] Anko Itosu (1831~1915) Motobu Choki (1870~1944) so this would have been around 1882 or 1883 and Itosu Sensei would have been about 51 or 52 years old.

二二

先生が自分の死に臨み、高弟の糸洲先生を枕頭に呼び「私は是迄で、力一ぱいに稽古をさせたが、實際の場合と言ふ事を一寸も考へず、自由と敏活を缺いで居る。今日になつて深くさとる處があるから、今後は足并松村について研究して呉れ」と遺言されたそうである。誠に心すべきことである。

繰り返して言ふが、稽古するには其の理を解して、基本の練習をやれば、自然と筋肉が練れて相常に噪くなるもので、運用と敏活と言ふ事を充分に理解しなければ何等のやにく立たない。

However when Nagahama Sensei was on his deathbed, he called his top student Itosu Sensei to his side and said to him,

All my life I have focused on doing training using as much power as I could generate, and I did not give a second thought to how this would be applied in a real situation, thus I gave no thought to freedom of movement and being nimble. Recently I have become enlightened to this fact so I strongly encourage you to study under Matsumura.

I believe this testament that Itosu Sensei left me should be taken to heart.

I may be repeating myself here, but when training you should discover the underlying principles of a technique. That combined with training the fundamentals will naturally allow you to strengthen your muscles and you will become very strong. If you do not have an understanding of how to manipulate your body and move quickly and deftly your technique will not benefit you.

ナイハンチの型と誤傳

ナイハンチで、足を八文字に開く型が有ることは、既に御承知のことゝ思ふ（ナイハンチ三圖參照）此際足のヒラをスボメて、内側に締付る様に力を入れることを現今普通一般に教へ、且つ世人も之れが正當の如く考へが、誤れるも甚だしい。此の型は専ら糸洲翁の流れを汲む方々の教へ方で、松村翁や佐久間翁などは、只足を八文字に開く丈けで力を取る様に教へられてゐた。此の點は自分も最初非常に疑問で、松村翁や佐久間翁に審したことがある。

松村翁は「糸洲の飄小型では、實際立ち合ふ場合には、頗る危險で、すぐ倒されてしまう」との御話であつた。つくゞ思ふに、私も松村翁の御說に從ひたいと思ふ。先づ試みに糸洲流で八文字に立ち、足の裏をスボメてみる人も背後から手の先で一寸押すと、容易く倒れる。斯くしては、如何に力を入れてかまへてゐても、何等の效果もない。型はなるべく實際に近い様に教ふべきもので、強いて力を入れんが爲めに、實際とかけはなれた型を世にのこすことは、餘り感心出來ないと思ふ。それで、自分は此の足の裏をスボメることには斷じて贅成出來ないと同時に、其の誤れることを敢て廣く世人に明かにしたい。

Naihanchi no Kata to Goden
Naihanchi and Misunderstandings Regarding This Kata

No doubt my readers are already aware that when doing the Kata Naihanchi your feet are in Hachimonji, or angled outwards like the bottom of the Kanji *Hachi* 八 meaning eight. (Please refer to picture three in the Naihanchi Kata.) These days when this technique is taught, students are typically instructed to focus their power on the inside the soles of their feet and push inward as if squeezing. However, though people of today think this is the proper way to do this technique, this is a mistake. This way of teaching the Kata is only done by those who have drunk in the flow of the venerable gentleman Itosu's teachings. The venerable gentleman Matsumura and the venerable gentleman Sakuma only teach that you should draw power just by sanding with your feet spread in Hachimonji.

I was initially quite dubious regarding this point so I asked both the venerable gentleman Matsumura and the venerable gentleman Sakamoto about it. The venerable gentleman Matsumura said,

Using Itosu's Kamiga Gata, Small Turtle Technique of standing, would be extremely dangerous in a real fight, you would almost immediately fall.

After considering this carefully I concluded that I am in agreement with the venerable gentleman Matsumura on this matter. First of all, I tried out the Itosu Ryu, Itosu Sensei style of standing. I stood in Hachimonji while putting an inward power in the soles of the feet. I found that if a person were to walk up from behind and push me in the back with their fingertips I would fall over easily. So no matter how you put power into this stance, it is not effective.

Kata should be taught in a manner that is as close to a realistic situation as possible and not be done as a method of increasing power. As for myself, I have no desire to leave behind techniques that are not applicable in a real-life situation. Thus, I feel that I cannot agree with the style of standing that focuses on putting power in the soles of the feet and pushing inward. At the same time I would like to make as many people as possible aware that this is a mistake.

二四

ナイハンの初段

ナイハンチは全部で三十三擧動よりなり便宜上一二三の號令を掛け順次動作す。

第 一 圖

用意の姿勢。

下腹部に力を入れ、姿勢を正しく、正面を見る。

この構へ方は全身力を入れ、護身の意を表せる型なり。

Naihanchi no Shodan
First Level of Naihanchi : Picture 1

Naihanchi consists of thirty-three separate movements. To simplify the instructions shouts of one, two, three… will be added.

Picture 1
Yoh-I no Shisei, Ready Position.

While keeping your posture straight and facing forward, focus power in your lower abdomen.

You should be standing with power filling your entire body. You are demonstrating that the meaning of this Kata is *Goshin*, protecting the body.

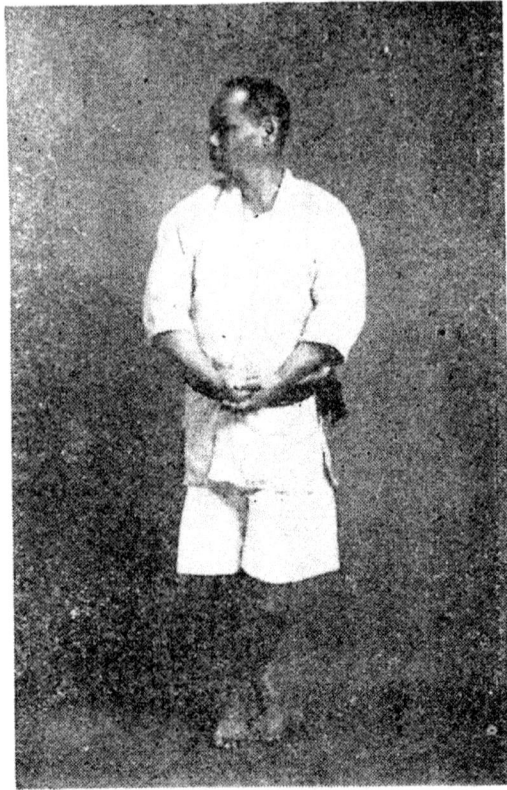

第　二　圖

膝頭を見ると同時に、常に輪く右
右側節を見ると同時に、左足は輕く右
足を越して、圖の如く、交叉す。但し
右側よりの攻撃を、一歩踏み込んで受
けると同時に、戰鬪開始の準備なり。

二五

Naihanchi no Shodan
First Level of Naihanchi : Picture 2

As the picture shows, look to the right and, at the same time, pass your left foot over the top of your right foot and place it lightly on the ground on the opposite side. This signifies you are stepping towards an opponent that is attacking you from the right while at the same time preparing to begin battle.

第三圖

二の呼稱で、右手を右へ伸ばすと同時に、右足を右へ岡の如く踏み出し、左手は握りながら脇腹に取り、充分後に引く、上體の姿勢はくずさず、腰に力を入れ、足は乘馬するが如く、兩脚の外側より中の方へ、力を締込むやうな心持で踏み張る、前述の通り、足の開備は一尺五寸位とす。目は敵を正視する。

この時打ち、伸ばしたる右手は、敵の攻撃を受けると同時に突き込み、而し型に變化したるを見よ、足の開備は一尺五寸位とす。目は敵を正視する。

て敵の手を握る意味を含む故手首より先は裏がへす様な動作をなすべし。足を踏み出すは、敵を蹴上る意たるべし。

Naihanchi no Shodan
First Level of Naihanchi : Picture 3

At the command of *Ni!* or Two! extend your right hand out to the right and, at the same time step out to the right with your right foot while making a fist with your left hand and bring it up by your *Waki-bara*, side under your armpit. This is shown in the picture.

Ensure that your left fist is pulled back sufficiently, your upper body remains upright and that you are not leaning one way or the other. You should focus power in your hips and stand as if you are mounted on a horse with the power in your legs. The image you should have in your mind is tightening your leg muscles from the outside focusing your power inward.

This is a variation of the previously mentioned Hachimonji stance. Observe how the feet are about 1 Shaku 5 Sun, 45 cm/ 18 in, apart. Your eyes should be focused directly on your opponent's face.

This strike with your extended right arm is simultaneously blocking your opponent's attack and hitting him.

第四圖

三の呼稱で、伸ばした手で摑まへて引寄するが如くに、同時に、左肘を以て敵を突く様に闆の如く動作す。但しこの時、肘を胸部より、五寸程はなし、上體は右向にし、下體をくずさぬ様注意すべし。實戰の場合は、右肘を以て突くにあらず、左の拳を以て突くべきものなり、型なればこそ、ていさいよく、かくせるなり、注意すべき事なり。

二七

Naihanchi no Shodan
First Level of Naihanchi : Picture 4

At the command of *San!* or Three! pull your extended right arm back as if you trying to yank it free after being grabbed. At the same time move your left elbow forward as if you are striking your opponent. This is shown in the picture.

Note that your elbow should extend about 5 Sun, 15 cm/ 6 inches, in front of your chest. Ensure that the lower half of your body remains stable and balanced while your upper body is twisted to the right.

In a Jissen, real fight, you would not strike with your elbow, rather you would hit with your left fist. Because this is a Kata, the true body movements are concealed. You should be aware of this point.

第　五　圖

四の呼稱で、拳と拳とを、右脇腹の處
に左を上に重ねると、同時に左側面を
見る。但しこの時體を正し、左肩が上
がらぬ様注意すべし。

これ左側面の攻撃に移る構へなり。

Naihanchi no Shodan
First Level of Naihanchi : Picture 5

At the command of *Yon!* or Four! shift both fists to your right side, with the left on top. At the same time turn and look to your left. Remember to maintain proper posture and be sure to not allow your left shoulder to rise.

At this point you are standing ready to face an attack from your left.

第 六 圖

五の呼稱で、前の姿勢をくづさず、其の
ま\左手を膝頭の前に打ちおろす。
敵、足を以て、蹴たほさんとせし故、
足をはらふ意なるべし。

二九

96

Naihanchi no Shodan
First Level of Naihanchi : Picture 6

At the command of *Go!* or Five! swing your left fist down in front of your left knee being careful not to disrupt the stance described on the previous page.

The reason this move is done is because your opponent tried to kick you in the leg, so you swept this attack away.

第 七 圖

六の呼稱で、左手を捻ち上げると同時に右手を圖の如く突き出し、上に重ねる。但し右の腕は、水の流れるが如く、肱より次第に拳を下げる。但し腕と胸との間隔は、見さ五寸位。

この型は側面の敵を突く意なるべし。

98

Naihanchi no Shodan
First Level of Naihanchi : Picture 7

At the command of *Roku!* or Six! twist your left hand up and simultaneously strike with your right hand so it ends up above your left as shown in the picture.

Your right fist should be slightly lower than your shoulder, just enough so that if water was poured onto your shoulder, it would flow downward towards your fist. Note that your right arm should be about 5 Sun, 15 cm/ 6 inches, in front of your chest.

The meaning of this portion of the Kata is attacking an opponent to your side.

第　八　圖

七の呼稱で、六の姿勢をくづさず、其の
まゝ右足を左足の上より輕く越して交
叉す。
但し側説へ進むの準備たり。

Naihanchi no Shodan
First Level of Naihanchi : Picture 8

At the command of *Nana!* or Seven! without breaking the stance you had in step six, pass your right foot over the top of your left foot and place it lightly on the ground on the opposite side. The meaning of this step is preparing to advance to the side.

第九圖

八の呼吸で、左足を一歩左へ開くと同
時に、右腕を圖の如く遯し、目は正面
に復す。但し拳は目より低く。面と拳
との離れは約一尺、脇と肘との離れ凡
そ五寸位と心得るべし。
膝を蹴る用ひは側面の敵を蹴たるもの
なるべし。

Naihanchi no Shodan
First Level of Naihanchi : Picture 9

At the command of *Hachi!* or Eight! step out to the left with your left foot. At the same time raise your right arm up as shown in the picture and return your eyes to facing front. Note that your fist should be below eye level. Your fist should be about 1 Shaku, 30 cm/ 12 inches, in front of your face while your elbow should be extended 5 Sun, 15 cm/ 6 inches, in front of your armpit.

The true meaning of the step out to your left is that you are aiming a kick at an opponent on your left side.

第十圖

九の呼稱と同時に、右手は下に打ち落し、左手は手先で鷗を描くが如く外側より上部に打ち上げ、上圖の如き姿勢となる。

此の間なるべく早きをたっとぶ。但し組手九圖はこの型の應用なり。

この型は敵のつゝ込み來るのを、我れ右手で下へ打ち落す。

Naihanchi no Shodan
First Level of Naihanchi : Picture 10

At the command of *Kyu!* or Nine! swing your right hand down in an Uchi Otoshi, dropping strike, while, at the same time, trace a circle with the end of your left hand moving outwards and up with an Uchi Age, rising strike, to the head. After this you should be positioned as shown in the picture.

These moves should all be done as fast as possible. The application for this move will become clear in Picture 9 of the Kumite section.

In this section of the Kata, you are using your right arm to knock down your opponent's attack with an Uchi Otoshi, dropping strike.

Kumite Picture 9

第十一圖

十の呼稱で姿勢をくづさず、左の拳を以て前面の敵の顏面をなぐるが如く、充分に打ち伸すと同時に、右の手首に左肘をのせる。同時に、左拳を以て敵の顏面をなぐる意なるべし。

Naihanchi no Shodan
First Level of Naihanchi : Picture 11

At the command of *Juu!* or Ten! swing your left fist forward to make as if you are hitting an opponent directly in front of you in the face. Be sure to maintain correct posture while you do this and extend your arm sufficiently. At the same time rest your left elbow on top of your right wrist.

The purpose of this move is to rapidly strike your opponent in the face.

第十二圖

十二の呼稱で、右腹膝を左側面を見ると同時に上圖の如く、左足を以て前面を掃ふが如くして、足を元の位置に復すこれ前面に蹴込む意たり。

三五

Naihanchi no Shodan
First Level of Naihanchi : Picture 12

At the command of *Juu-ichi!* or Eleven! look to the left and simultaneously use your left leg to Harau, sweep, the area in front of you, then return your foot to its original position. The meaning of this is you are responding to a front kick.

第十三圖

十二の呼稱で、上體を左に捻て側面より突いて來るのを受ける。

この時、よく腕を捻ぢる様に教へる人あるも、誤れるも甚だし、何んとなれば手の甲を以て受る決無し、注意すべし。

Naihanchi no Shodan
First Level of Naihanchi : Picture 13

At the command of *Juu-ni!* or Twelve! twist your upper body so you are facing left and block the strike coming from that direction.

There are people that teach that when blocking you should twist your arm as much as possible, however many people misinterpret this. It is important to understand that there is no method of blocking with the back of the hand.

第十四圖

十三の呼稱で、右側面を見ると同時に
十二圖と同じく右足を以て、前面を拂
ふ如くし、足を元の位置に復す。
足を拂ふは、前面に蹴込む意なり。

Naihanchi no Shodan
First Level of Naihanchi : Picture 14

At the command of *Juu-san!* or Thirteen! look to the right and, at the same time, sweep your right leg inward the same way you did in Picture 12, then return your leg to its previous position.

The reason you are sweeping your leg like this is because your opponent has kicked to your front.

第十五圖

十四の呼稱で、上圖の如く、右側面よ
り突いて來るのを上體を捻つて受ける
従手は防護の意とす。

Naihanchi no Shodan
First Level of Naihanchi : Picture 15

At the command of *Juu-yon!* or Fourteen! twist your upper body to block an attack from your right side. This is shown in the picture. The purpose of your right arm is to serve as protection.

第十六圖

十五の呼稱で、拳と拳とを圖の如く、右脇腹の處に左を上に重ねると同時に、右側面を見る。但し肩が上がらぬ樣、注意。

これ次の動作の準備なり。

Naihanchi no Shodan
First Level of Naihanchi : Picture 16

At the command of *Juu-go!* or Fifteen! move both fists to your right side, with your left fist on top. At the same time look to your left.[8] However be careful not to allow your left shoulder to rise.

This is setting you up for the next movement.

---

[8] The text says "right" however the picture shows Motobu Choki looking to his left.

第十七圖

十六の呼稱で、重ねたる兩手を、姿勢をくづさず右側面に突き出す。

これより突き込まれたるを受ける意、所謂夫婦手を形化せるなり。

Naihanchi no Shodan
First Level of Naihanchi : Picture 17

At the command of *Juu-roku!* or Sixteen! strike to your left with both fists, staggered high and low, being sure not to allow your balance to crumble.

The meaning of this part of the Kata is defending against your opponent's attack from your left. It is Mefutote, Husband and Wife Hands, as seen in a Kata.[9]

---

[9] Motobu Choki writes it as Mefutode (due to old Kana usage this would probably have been read as Meutode,) however it is generally written as Meotode these days.

第十八圖

十七の正鵠と共に、右手を右脇腹の處
に強く引くと同時に左手を上に捻りな
がら手を圖の如く開く。
左手で敵を摑む意なるべし。

Naihanchi no Shodan
First Level of Naihanchi : Picture 18

At the command of *Juu-nana!* or Seventeen! pull your right fist forcefully back and place it on your right side, below your armpit. At the same time, rotate your left hand up and open it as shown in the picture.

The left hand in this position indicates you seized your opponent.

第十九圖

十八の呼稱と共に、闊の如く上體を左
へ捻り右肘を使つて突く。但し下體の
姿勢を崩さぬやう注意すべし。

Naihanchi no Shodan
First Level of Naihanchi : Picture 19

At the command of *Juu-hachi!* or Eighteen! do as shown in the picture, namely twist your upper body to the left and strike with your right elbow. Be sure not to allow your lower body to become unbalanced.

第二十圖

十九の呼稱で、正面を見ると同時に、兩手を左脇腹の處に上圖の如く組む。

Naihanchi no Shodan
First Level of Naihanchi : Picture 20

At the command of *Juu-kyu!* or Nineteen! turn and face forward while at the same time bringing both hands to your left side under your armpit. This is shown in the picture.

第二十二圖
二十の呼稱と同時に、右側面を見て、
右手を圖の如く、打ちおとす。

四四

Naihanchi no Shodan
First Level of Naihanchi : Picture 21

As soon as you hear the command of *Nijuu!* or Twenty! turn to the right and strike with an Uchi Otoshi, dropping strike, with your right hand.

第二十二圖
三十一の呼稱で、圖の如く右脇腹に、
兩手を組む。

四五

128

Naihanchi no Shodan
First Level of Naihanchi : Picture 22

At the command of *Nijuu-ichi!* or Twenty-one! position both hands by your right side as shown in the picture.

第二十三圖

二十二の呼稱で、姿勢を崩さず右側に移動する準備として、左足を右足の上に輕く越して交叉す。

四六

Naihanchi no Shodan
First Level of Naihanchi : Picture 23

At the command of *Nijuu-ni!* or Twenty-two! pass your left foot over the top of your right foot and place it lightly on the ground on the opposite side in order to set yourself up to move to the right. Be sure to sure to remain in a stable stance.

第二十四図

二十三の呼称と、同時に、右足を一歩

右側に踏み出す、足と足との間隔は、

約一尺五寸より二尺位とす。

四七

Naihanchi no Shodan
First Level of Naihanchi : Picture 24

As soon as you hear the command of *Nijuu-san!* or Twenty-three! step out to the right with your right foot. The distance between your feet should be from 1 Shaku 5 Sun to 2 Shaku, 45~60 cm/ 1.5~2 feet.

第二十五圖

二十四の呼稱で、正面を見ると同時に左手を圖の如く起す。但し拳は目より少し下位につ肩との間、約一尺五寸位にし、前面よりの攻撃を内受する意たるべし。

Naihanchi no Shodan
First Level of Naihanchi : Picture 25

At the command of *Nijuu-yon!* or Twenty-four! turn to the front and, at the same time, raise your left fist up as shown in the picture. Note that your fist should be slightly lower than eye level. Your fist should be about 1 Shaku 5 Sun, 45cm/ 18 inches, in front of your shoulders.

The meaning of this part of the Kata is stopping a front attack with an Uchi Uke, inner block.

第二十六圖

二十五の呼稱と同時に、右手を右肩の
前より、打ち下し、左手を左肩の外側
より打ち上げる氣持ちで、敏速に動作
し、圖の如き姿勢になる。

四九

Naihanchi no Shodan
First Level of Naihanchi : Picture 26

As soon as you hear the command of *Nijuu-go!* or Twenty-five! swing your left hand towards the front of your right shoulder and down in an Uchi Oroshi, dropping strike. Your right hand swings up towards your left shoulder in an Uchi Age, rising strike. Your right hand should feel like it is moving to the outside of your left shoulder.

These movements should all be executed quickly and you should be positioned as shown in the picture at the end.

第三十七圖

二十六の呼稱で、左腕を圖の如く、前
面に構へ同時に右手の肘をささゐると
共に、右腕を充分に前方に、打ち伸し
て元の位置に復す。

五〇

138

Naihanchi no Shodan
First Level of Naihanchi : Picture 27

At the command of *Nijuu-roku!* or Twenty-six! move your left arm forward so it is positioned as shown in the picture. You are now standing facing forward with your left hand supporting your right elbow. Strike forward with your right fist, ensuring you extend your right arm forward sufficiently and then return to this position.

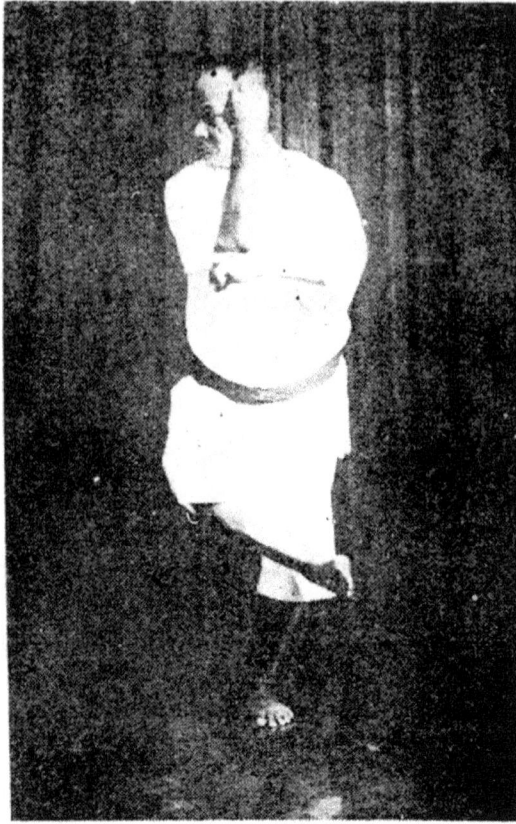

第二十八図

二十七の呼稱で、右側面を見て姿勢を崩さず右足を以て図の如く前面を蹴上るやうに挑ひ、足を元の位置に復す。

Naihanchi no Shodan
First Level of Naihanchi : Picture 28

At the command of *Nijuu-nana!* or Twenty-seven! look to your right and sweep your right leg to your left and up, being careful to maintain your balance. This is shown in the picture. Then return your leg to its original position.

第二十九圖

二十六の呼稱で右足を右側に捻じ下
し體を崩さず右側よりの攻擊を受る。

五二

142

Naihanchi no Shodan
First Level of Naihanchi : Picture 29

At the command of *Nijuu-hachi!* or Twenty-eight! turn your upper body to the right, while ensuring your lower body remains stable. You are blocking an attack from your right side.

第三十圖

二十九の呼稱で、左側面を見て左足を
以て前面を蹴上る如く拂ひて足を元の
位置に復す。

五三

144

Naihanchi no Shodan
First Level of Naihanchi : Picture 30

At the command of *Nijuu-kyu!* or Twenty-nine! look to your left, and sweep your foot to your right to avoid a kick from your left side before returning your foot to its original position.

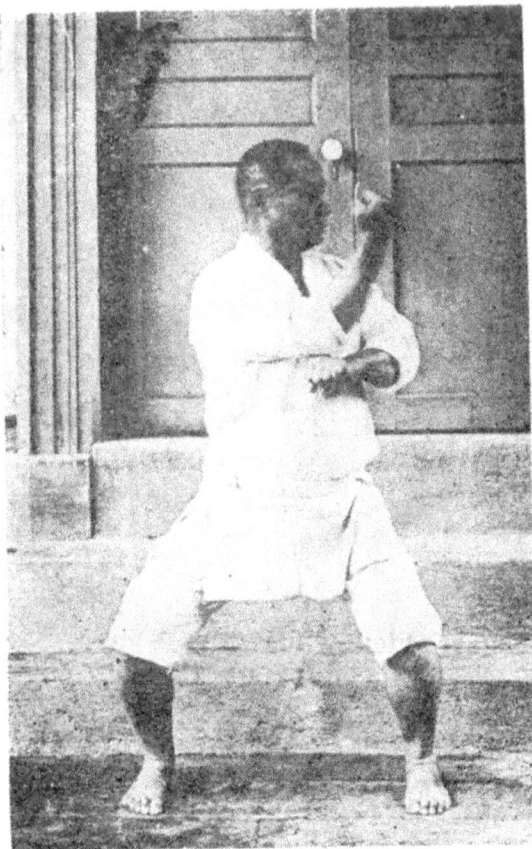

第三十一圖

三十の呼稱で、上體を左側に捻じ左側
よりの攻撃を受るやうに圖の如く腕も
ろ共に廻す。

五四

Naihanchi no Shodan
First Level of Naihanchi : Picture 31

At the command of *Sanjuu!* or Thirty! turn your upper body to the left in order to block an attack from that side. Your arms should rotate in unison with your body.

第三十二圖

三十一の呼稱で、前面を見ると共に、腕を圖の如く、左脇腹に構へる。

Naihanchi no Shodan
First Level of Naihanchi : Picture 32

At the command of *Sanjuu-ichi!* or Thirty-one! turn to face the front and at the same time bring both hands beside your left side. This is shown in the picture.

第三十三圖
三十三の姿勢で、右側面を見て、左右
兩手を場に突き出す。

五六

Naihanchi no Shodan
First Level of Naihanchi : Picture 33

At the command of *Sanjuu-ni!* or Thirty-two! look to your right and strike with both fists.

第三十四圖

三十三の呼稱で、右足を引くと同時に正面を見作ら両手を引ひて最初の姿勢に復す。

五七

Naihanchi no Shodan
First Level of Naihanchi : Picture 34

At the command of *Sanjuu-san!* or Thirty-three! pull your right foot beside your left and at the same time face forward as you bring both hands together, returning to the starting stance.

かまへの心得

普通能くかまへといふて、種々型が有るが、是は一片の形式である事を、承知して置いて貰ひたい。然らばといつて、全然排斥すべきものではない。實戰の場合には、必ず左様にかまへるべきものかと問ふ人が有つたら、否然らず、かまへに形ち無しと申したい。余は心にかまへはあると主張するのである。臨機應變、とつさの場合に處する心掛けが、平日から肝要で、是のかまへが好いとかあのかまへ方が好いとか一概に申さるべきものではない。要はたゞ、平日から武力を練ると同時に、精神を練るにあるので、大いに心すべきことである。

Kamae no Kokoroe
Lessons Regarding Kamae

It is typically said that there are many different kinds of Kamae, or stances. However I would like my readers to understand that this is simply a formal way to refer to them. That being said I am not recommending they be rejected. When someone asks me, "What Kamae do you take in a fight?" I invariably respond, "I take a Kamae without shape." What this means is that my mind is in Kamae.

It is important that you are able to respond to a sudden danger with *Rin-Ki-O-Hen* 臨機応変 reacting and adapting according to the situation. It is essential that this is part of your daily training instead of saying, "I like this Kamae, or I like that Kamae." Thus I advise that as you are training your martial skills on a daily basis, you need to be aware that it is extremely important to be forging your mental acuity at the same time.

唐手に先手なし

「唐手に先手なし」といふ言葉が有る、人によつては、其まゝ文字通り解釈して、能く「先手してはいけない」と教へる方々がある様だが、余程考へ違いをしてゐると思ふ。たるほど、武道精神といふものは、決してみだりに人をたぐる為めに稽古するものではない。心身の鍛練が、第一の目的でなければならない事は、既に承知してゐる事と思ふ。そこで、此の言葉は、やたらに危害を加へてはいけないとふ意味であつて、余儀ない場合、即ちさけてもさけられぬ場合、敵が頂に危害を加へんとする場合には、猛然と立つて戦はなければならぬ。苟く戦ひに臨みては、敵を制することが肝要で、敵を制するには、最初の一手で制して貰かれねばならぬ。だから戦ひに臨みては、先手でなければならぬ。大きに心すべきことである。

156

Karate Sente Nashi
Karate Practitioners Do Not Strike First

Regarding the phrase *Karate Sente Nashi*, some people interpret this directly as "Karate practitioners should never strike first." While there are people that teach that interpretation of the phrase, I feel that they are completely in error. I have already discussed how *Shin Shin Tanren*, forging both the mind and body, should be your primary goal when training.

There is an inherent danger that has to be considered to understand this phrase. If you have been forced into a situation where our opponent is intent on causing you harm, you have no choice but to fight ferociously.

In the end when you are in a situation where you will have to fight, it is essential that you control your opponent. By controlling your opponent I am referring to suppressing his initial attack. Thus, when in a situation where you will have to fight, you must make the first move. This is an important lesson to take to heart.

組 手

　琉球拳法唐手は、基本と組手の二つに分つことが出來る。基本とは、唐手の基をなすので、俗に型と稱へ、（ナイハンチ、パッサイ等）初心者にもこれをよく教へるのであるが、組手は柔道に於けるキメの型にやや似て、一齣づゝ連續的になつて居り、琉球語の手を組むといふことから轉訛して組手と稱するやうになつたものと思はれる。尤も組手は、琉球に於ては、古來より行はれたのであるが、未だ一定した型といふものなく、尚ほ支那にも殘つてゐないのである。そして組手に對する參考書と稱するものもあるが、その多くは支那の武人が編成したものを書寫して武人仲間に珍重がられたもので、琉球獨特の組手は實に未だ編成されてゐない。元來唐手は剛術であるため其の技が未だ充分でない人には試みることすら危險が伴ふのであつて、一通り基本の教習を卒へた人が互に受けはづしを試みて、稽古することが出來るのである。そのため人に依つて色々變化をするものであつて決して制定した組手といふものはないのである。されば組手を稽古せんとする人は、常に敏捷を旨として相手を選び、よく「受けはづす」ことを稽古すれば自と組手の稽古をしたことになるから、自らの技を上達を期するのが、尤も肝要なことであらうと思はれる。

Kumite
Paired Training

Ryukyu Kenpo Karate can be divided into two sections; Kihon, fundamentals, and Kumite, paired training. Kihon forms the base of Karate and the techniques that make up the Kihon are known colloquially as Kata. These (Kata such as Naihanchi, Passai and so on) are frequently taught to new students, however Kumite is done in a manner that is quite similar to the Kime no Kata of Judo[10] since they are done one after another in a continuous sequence.

---

[10] *Kime no Kata* 極の形 is a series of twenty Judo Kata. The series consists of two parts: eight seated techniques and twelve standing techniques. These include defending against both armed and unarmed opponents.

Translator's Note: Kime no Kata

Instructor's Guide to the Fundamentals of Kendo and Judo 剣柔一体武道の基礎的指導 Takashima Yoshio 1943	
Judo Kime no Kata : *Kiri Oroshi*, Cutting down	
切　下 （飛ひ込んで制し當てたところ）	切　下 （腹固を行つた所）
Leap forward and strike your opponent in the face while controlling his arm.	Lock his arm against your stomach.

The term used for this paired training "Kumite" is thought to be derived from a corruption of a word in the Ryukyu language that means "to join the hands together."

Kumite has been trained from ancient times in Ryukyu, and there was not any prescribed form to it, however no documents related to this method of training survived to the present day. While there are some books that seem to be related to Kumite training these are for the most part compiled by Chinese martial artists and are copied by fellow martial artists, who treasure them highly. However these do not contain the true information regarding the Kumite particular to the Ryukyu islands.[11]

From the very beginning Karate is a Go Ryu, strong style of fighting, meaning that even people with very little technique can still be quite dangerous. After you receive training in the fundamentals you should work with a partner and try blocking and deflecting strikes. From that point you can begin doing Keiko, training. However people will change and alter things in many ways so there is no clearly defined Kumite no Kata, or Paired Training With Prescribed Actions.

That being said, the primary focus for anyone seeking to do Kumite training should be to find a partner that is nimble and quick. If you focus on Uke Hazusu, blocking and deflecting, when training you can be assured that your technique will steadily improve. I believe this is a fundamental aspect of training.

---

[11] Motobu Choki is probably referring to the Bubishi. An example of how these Kumite Kata were introduced is included on the following page.

Translator's Note: Bubishi

Bubishi
Date Unknown. This version was owned by Mabuni Kenwa
(1889 ~1952) and copied by Fujita Seiko (1898~1966)

錦鯉朝王手敗

美女梳粧手勝

Left: Carp Using Rising To Tomorrow Technique: Loses
Right: Woman Running A Comb Through Her Hair : Wins

The ornamental carp uses Rising To Tomorrow strikes. You respond with Beautiful Woman Running Her Comb Through Her Hair. You grab his hair and pull down while your other hand comes up from below to his jaw. Twist and break in a clean motion. It is said this will result in your opponent's defeat.

本部朝基・MOTOBU CHOKI

組手
Kumite
Paired Training

第 一 圖

相手が右手を以て胸ぐらをつかんだ時、
左手を以て相手の手首を下方より握る

相手が顔面を突かんとした時、少しか
ゞみ、右腕を深くつゝ込みて受上げる
と同時に、

Kumite
Paired Training : Picture 1

Your opponent reaches out with his right hand and seizes your Mune-gura, collar. You respond by grabbing his wrist from below with your left hand. When he tries to punch you in the face, crouch down slightly. Drive your right arm in deep to block and also force your opponent's arm up. At the same time…

第 二 圖

第二の如く相手の手首を強く引くと共に右拳を以て相手の胸下を突けば勝となる。

左手で胸ぐらをつかんだ時亦同じ。

Kumite
Paired Training : Picture 2

...do as shown in the second picture. Yank your opponent's wrist and, at the same time strike him in Mune-shita, lower chest. You have won the bout.

If you begin this Kata with the opponent grabbing your collar with his left hand, the technique progresses in the same way.

第 三 圖

相手が、前と同様に、右手を以て胸ぐらをつかんだ時、左手を以て相手の手首を下方より握り、右手を以て腕を握り強く引き寄せると同時に。

Kumite
Paired Training : Picture 3

Your opponent reaches out with his right hand and seizes your
Mune-gura, collar. You respond by grabbing his wrist from below
with your left hand. When he tries to punch you in the face, crouch
down slightly. Drive your right arm in deep to block and force your
opponent's arm up. At the same time…

第四圖

六四

圖の如く、右手の指を延ばしたまゝ圖の如く手双を以に相手の脇腹をなぐる。但し左手を以って胸ぐらをつかんだ時亦同じ。（勝手）

Kumite
Paired Training : Picture 4

...do as the fourth picture shows. While keeping the fingers of your right hand extended, strike your opponent in the Waki Bara, side under the armpit, with a Te Gatana, Sword Hand. Note that your left hand is still holding onto your opponent's wrist like in the previous step. (This move seals your victory.)

第　五　圖

前圖と同じく、胸ぐらをつかんだ時、
同じく右手を以て相手の手首を握り、
少し體をかはしてそとにそらす。

Kumite
Paired Training : Picture 5

Your opponent seizes your collar, just as shown in the first picture of the previous technique. Grip your opponent's wrist with your right hand and rotate your body slightly clockwise to the outside to evade your opponent's attack.

第六圖

相手は非常に不利の立場になる、相手の右手を強く引くと同時に、左拳を以て圖の如く横胸を突く。

176

Kumite
Paired Training : Picture 6

Your opponent is now in an extremely disadvantageous position.
Yank hard on his left arm as you strike to Yoko Mune, the side of
the chest.

第 七 圖

相手猶ひるまず、左拳を以て突かんと
する時、相手の手首を充分に引きなが
ら、左手をつつ込んだ圖の如く、相手
の左腕をおさへること恰も弓を引く氣
持で左肩の腕を引くべし。相手猶ひる
まざれば、相手の手首を下に押すと同
時に自分の左腕を上げれば相手の腕は
折れるべし。

六七

Kumite
Paired Training : Picture 7

Despite your reaction, your opponent does not hesitate and attacks again with his left fist. Respond as shown in the picture by yanking hard on his right wrist while driving your left hand forward. This will Osae, or suppress, your opponent's left arm. One arm is pushing and the other arm is pulling as if you are drawing a bow.

If your opponent still continues his attack, push his right wrist down while raising your left arm. This will break his arm.

第 八 圖

相手が左拳にて我顔へ突き來る時、右腕を深くつつ込みて圖の如くして受けはづす。この時左手は豫備として右手に附ておく。

六八

Kumite
Paired Training : Picture 8

Your opponent tries to punch you in the face with his left fist. Respond by driving in deep with your right arm, blocking his attack and knocking his arm aside. This is shown in the picture. When doing this place your left hand against your right arm in case it is needed.

第　九　圖

相手たば右手を以て突きくる時、我れ
左手を以て打ち落して受け、右拳を以
て相手の顏面をたくる。

六九

Kumite
Paired Training : Picture 9

Your opponent attacks with his right hand. You respond by using Uchi Otoshi, Dropping Strike, with your right hand and punching him in the face with your left fist.

第 十 圖

互に右手を組み、横へて居る時、相手
左拳を以て横腹を突き來る。

Kumite
Paired Training : Picture 10

   Both you and your opponent press your right arms together. From this stance your opponent strikes to Yoko Bara, side of your stomach, with his left fist.

第十一圖

其の時上體を少しかわして、上圖の如く受けると同時に、右手拳を以て突き來る時、左手を以て內受す、尤も左手を豫備として常に右手に付けてたければはとても受けらるべきものにあらず。

Kumite
Paired Training : Picture 11

As the picture shows, twist your upper body slightly clockwise as you block this with your right hand. As your opponent strike with his right hand, use your left hand to block this with an Uchi Uke, inside block. If you do not make a habit of keeping your left hand against your right hand Yobi, ready in reserve, then you will not be able to block this attack.

第十二圖

受けたら、すぐ圖の如く兩腕を握り、
ひざを以て相手の睾を突く。

七二

Kumite
Paired Training : Picture 12

As soon as you have blocked your opponent's arms, seize both his arms and knee him in the groin. This is shown in the picture.

第十三圖

相手突き來たら、受けるとすぐ左手で首を握り上げ、右足を踏み込み右手を以て踵を握る。

Kumite
Paired Training : Picture 13

When your opponent attacks with a punch, block it with your left hand and then immediately grab his wrist and force it up. Step forward with your right foot and seize his testicles with your right hand.

第十四圖

左手首を撮り上げると同時に、右足を踏み込み、肘を曲て圖の如く胸を突く。

Kumite
Paired Training : Picture 14

You are stepping forward with your right foot and lifting your opponent's left wrist up at the same time. Strike him in the Mune, chest, with your elbow as shown in the illustration.

第十五圖

我が顔を突き來る時、我れ上體を相手
の右側にそらし、外受して相手の脇腹
を突く。

Kumite
Paired Training : Picture 15

Your opponent attacks with a punch to your face. You respond by twisting your body counterclockwise and blocking his attack with a Soto Uke, outside block, with your right hand and strike him in Waki Bara, side under the armpit, with your left hand.

第十六圖

相手の左拳を以て突き來る時、矢張り
體をかはして左腕を以て外受し、尚左
足を以て蹴込みたる時、矢張右手を打
ち下して受け、右手を以て横腹を突く。

Kumite
Paired Training : Picture 16

Your opponent attacks with a left punch. In this technique as well you twist your body and use your left arm to do a Soto Uke, outside block.

Your opponent responds with a left kick which you also block with a Uchi Oroshi, dropping strike, with your left hand. Finally, strike to your opponent's Yoko Bara, side of the stomach, with your right hand.

第十七圖
君と君とを組める時、相手右拳を以て
突き來る時、棍で受想

七七

Kumite
Paired Training : Picture 17

This technique starts off with your right arm and your opponent's right arm braced against each other. Your opponent attacks with a right punch.

第十八圖

急に上體を捻じ、左手を以て相手の右手を外より受けかへると、すきが生ずる故、すぐ胸を突くべし。

Kumite
Paired Training : Picture 18

Respond by rapidly twisting your upper body and use your left arm to block your opponent's right punch to the outside. This will create an opening in your opponent's defenses so immediately strike him in Mune, the chest.

第十九圖
後より不意にだきしめられたる時。

七九

Kumite
Paired Training : Picture 19

An attacker unexpectedly wraps his arms around you from behind.

第二十圖

両腕を張るが如く力を入れて、少し腰
を据るとゆるみが出る故、圖の如く手
をまわして襟を掴る。

八〇

Kumite
Paired Training : Picture 20

Respond by flexing both arms, putting all your power in them while dropping your hips slightly. This will create a small opening for you to turn your arm around and grip your opponent's testicles. This is shown in the picture.

本部朝基・MOTOBU CHOKI

Ryukyu no Umeru Bujin to Sono Tokugi

琉球の産める武人と其の特技

Warriors that Ryukyu Gave Birth to and Their Specialty

琉球の生める武人こそその特技

琉球の拳法唐手は、傳統的のもので、何時の頃より、克くこれを研鑽せるかといふ事に就ては、本存の琉球の文献にもなく且つ之が考證となるべき何ものもない。茲に列傳的にものする武人傳も、實に著者が古老より聞き傳へたる、三百年來の武人に過ぎないのである。之を年代順に列記すれば、首里では、西平親方、佛侶通頎、具志川親方、渡嘉敷親雲上、唐手佐久川、宣野灣朝内、血緣チャーン、宇久田、松元、汀志良次の棒宮里、關羽佐渡山で、降つて泄堅ハンタ小、北谷屋良、太田接司、大田ノ長小樽、上庶、松村、赤平の石嶺、外間、本村、崎原、油屋山城、當間親雲上、野村、棒名城、下中箇、寒川の石嶺の順で、ごく近世になつて大城、金城、多和田、豐見城親方、佐久間、喜屋武、國頭、添石親方、牧志、糸洲、安里、筑佐事、儀間等で、那覇では其志、崎山、長濱、桑江等が著名た武人であつた。

尚ほその外、泊の松茂良、親泊、山田の三人にがあり、久米に、村山、城間村に棒古波藏、古波藏村に宮平といふ突手の名人が控へて居たのである。

Ryukyu no Umeru Bujin to Sono Tokugi
Warriors that Ryukyu Gave Birth to and Their Specialty

Kenpo Karate is the traditional art of the Ryukyu islands. However, if you were to try and research when this tradition began you would find that there are no extant Ryukyu documents nor are there any artifacts available for study. This section will include some biographies of famous martial artists based stories told to the author by elderly people knowledgeable about events in the distant past. However the tales of these warriors only extend back about three hundred years.

If we look at these in chronological order, the earliest are the men from Shuri:

Nishinda Oyakata, the monk Tsushin, Gushichikawa Oyakata, Tokashiki Pe-chin, Karate Sakugawa, Ginowan Donchi, Makabe Chaanga, Ukuda, Matsumoto, Bo Miyazato from Choshiraji, Kan-u and Sadoyama.

Later came: Tsuken Hantaga, Chantan Yara, Ota Ansu, Ota No Nagasutaruu, Uehara, Matsumura, Ishimine from Akahira, Hokama, Motomura, Sakihara, Andaya Yamagusuku, Toma Pe-chin, Nomura, Bonagusuku, Shichanakausunme- and Ishimine from Sunga-.

Quite recently there were people such as Ohgusuku, Kanagusuku, Tawada, Toyomigusuku Oyakata, Tamashiro Oyakata, Sakuma, Kyan, Kunjan, Suishi Oyakata, Makishi, Itosu, Asato, Chikusaji and Gima as well as others.

There were well-known martial artist residing in Naha such as Gushi, Sakiyama, Nagahama and Kuwae as well as others.

In addition to the above, there were experts of *Tsukite* 突手 striking, such as Matsumura, Oyadomari and Yamada from Tomari and Murayama from Kume, Bo Kohagura from Gusukuma village and Miyadaira from Kohagura village.

In addition to the above, there were innumerable self-proclaimed Karate Tatsujin, experts at Chinese Hand.

The following section will introduce famous warriors and their special technique. These are not chronological order.

Translator's Note: Oyakata (Ueekata)

Oyakata (Ueekata) Fufu[12]

---

[12] "Oyakata" is a term for the highest rank of a non-noble aristocrat in the Ryukyu Kingdom. While in the Ryukyu language it is pronounced Ueekata, this book writes the word as "Oyakata."

Hyakusho Fufu
Peasant Couple

-Illustrated Guide to Ryukyu Traditions and Culture 琉球風俗図
-19th century

尚ほその他にも、十把一束の所謂、自稱唐手の達人は數へきれない程あった。今各人に就き、其の特技を紹介

すれば（年代順序等不同）

西平親方は、俗に佐部の親方と稱し、現居首里儀保の西平の先祖で、唐手の外に槍をよくしたといふ。

具志川親方は、唐手の達人であったと同時に、木刀の名人で、當時琉球の劍術家であった。

逆眞は、今より約三百年前の人で西平時代の武人で、唐に於て斯道の研鑚を積み、身は偏侶であり乍ら、當時に於て琉球の武人仲間でも一二を爭つたといふ、而も彼は凡ゆる武術に秀で、人を膁する程の力量があつたと傳へられる。

渡嘉敷親雲上は、人も知る琉球隨一の奇人で、武人といふよりも寧ろその奇行を以て知られてゐる。彼は又狂歌をよくし、德利を手の掌で一擊のもとに打ちくだいたといふ。

唐手佐久川は、琉球の過去における、所謂武道の一劃線とも稱さるべき人で、彼の後には彼なく、後世の世に稱せらるゝ人で、力技その他の點に於いて、彼の右に出る程の人はなかった。而も彼は人も知る如く、三角飛びの名人で、人と立ち合ふ時など、目にモノ見せぬ程の早技で、三角の壁を此のゆるみもなく蹴上げ

Martial Artists During the Era of:

King Sho Kei 尚敬王 (1700 ~1752)

Nishinda Oyakata was commonly called Sabi no Oyakata. He was the forefather of the Nishinda line presently residing in Shuri Gibo. In addition to Karate it is said he was skilled with the Yari, spear.

Gushikawa Oyakata was both a Karate expert and a master of fighting with the Bokuto, wooden sword. He was a Kenjutsu-ka, sword fighting master in Ryukyu at that time.

Tsushin lived three hundred years ago. He was a warrior alive at the same time as Nishinda no Oyakata. He worked diligently over a long period to develop a new approach to Chinese style martial arts. Though he was a monk, he was in competition with his fellow martial artists for either the best warrior or the second best warrior. Further, he excelled at other martial arts as well and it is said he was able to overpower anyone with his strength.

Martial Artists During the Era of:
King Sho Boku 尚穆王 (1739 ~ 1794)
King Sho On 尚温王 (1784 ~ 1802)

Tokashiki Pe-chin is said to have been known as the greatest eccentric of Ryukyu. He was known for his eccentricity rather than for being a martial artist. He also frequently wrote Kyoka, satirical poems, and it is said he could crack a ceramic Tokuri sake bottle with one strike of his palm.

Karate Sakugawa is the man who should be thought of as the one who drew a line from the martial arts of Ryuku's past to the present. Even later generations declared there was no one like him. Regarding his strength, it was said that there was no one that could match him. It is said he was well-regarded as a master of the *Sankaku Tobi*, triangle jump, and when he faced off against a person he moved so fast it wouldn't register in the eye. The way he could kick his way up three points on a wall without slipping showed his almost fearful skill.

Translator's Note: Ryukyu Spears and Polearms

Personal Record of the Ryukyu Kingdom 琉球國私記 1832
By Takai Bankei 高井伴寛 (1762~1838)

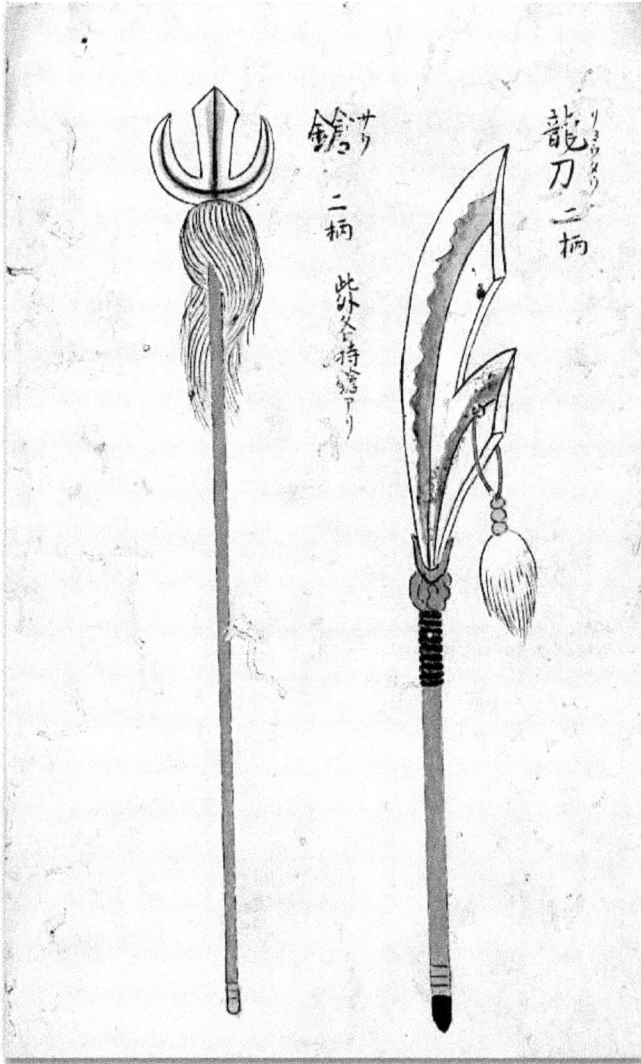

R: *Illustration of one of two Ryuto, Dragon Sword tipped spears*
L: *Illustration of one of two So-, spears*
There are other spears as well

て平然たりとは、寶に恐るべきである。池城ハンタ小、下中祝は、棒の達人として知られてゐる。

宜灣殿內は、有名な宜灣朝保の父君で、軆軀巨大、身の丈六尺三寸餘、軆重實に三百三十有餘斤で、怪力の持主として當時の人に稱はれ、七寸廻りの長サ七尺餘の輿の棒でツバメを打ち落す術に長じてゐた。彼宜灣が正しく膝まづく時は、悠に大人一人をかくすことが出來たとのことである。

眞壁チャーン小は、身の丈五尺三寸、軆軀肥滿の人で、一見鈍重な人と見えたが、武を練つた人だけに、チャーン小、の異名がよく示す如く小々身が輕く、あだかも雄鷲（チャーン）の樣に前後左右に飛び廻つたといふ。現に眞壁御殿は、當時のまんま家屋敷も殘つてゐるが、同家の表座敷の天井には、昔彼が足裏に油をつけて蹴り上げた跡方が未だに殘つてゐるのを見る、如何に彼が身輕く飛切の術に長じてゐたかといふことが點頭かれるであらう。

關羽佐渡山は、その名の恋す如く美貌の持主で、古、の唐の關羽もかくあらんと言はれた程、關羽に似通へる所があつたといふ。而も彼は唐手をよくすると共に、槍の名人としても聞えてゐる。

上原は、釵の名人であつた。

八三

Tsuken Hantaga and Shikyanaka Usumii were both famous as Bo no Tatsujin, masters of the wooden staff.

Giwan Donchi is the father of the famous Giwan Choho. He was a giant man who stood 6 Shaku 3 Sun, 189 cm/ 6'2" and he weighed more than 230 Kin, 138 kilograms/ 304 pounds. He possessed a fearful strength that people at the time found quite unusual. He would demonstrate a technique where he would knock a flying swallow from the sky using a palanquin pole that was 7 Shaku long and 7 Sun in circumference. (2.1 meters long 21 cm around, 6'11" long 2' 4 inches around.)

It is said that when Giwan sat down in Seiza, with his legs tucked under him, it was possible for an adult to hide behind him without being seen from the front.

Makabe Chaanga was a fat man who stood 5 Shaku 3 Sun, 160 cm/ 5'2", and appeared slow-witted. However since he had trained martial arts extensively, he had earned the nickname Chaanga due to the way he could move his body lightly. Chaan is the word for "rooster" in the Ryukyu dialect. He was so named for his ability to jump forward, back, left or right all while turning.

Even today the Makabe manor house remains unchanged from olden times. However if you look at the ceiling of the front parlor you can see his footprints on the ceiling. Long ago he brushed oil on his feet and kicked upward, marking the ceiling. I think we can all agree that this is evidence Makabe mastered the art of jumping.[13]

---

[13] In the lineage chart this man is listed as Morishima Oyakata, however in this description he is called Makabe Chaanga.

Kanu Sadoyama. As his name suggests, he had a fantastic beard that recalled the ancient Chinese warrior Guan Yu (?~220 AD) who was famous for his beard.[14] It is said Kanu resembled Guan Yu. He is said to have been a skilled Karate practitioner as well as a famously skilled with the spear.

Uehara was famous for his skill with the Sai.

---

[14] The name Kanu 関羽 is read as "Guan Yu" in Chinese. Guan Yu (?~220 AD) was a Chinese military general serving under the warlord Liu Bei during the late Eastern Han dynasty of China. While there are no paintings or descriptions of Guan Yu's physical appearance, the *The Records of the Three Kingdoms* records him as having a "peerless beard." There is a 19th century woodblock print of him on the following page.

Portrait of Kanu
by Katsukawa Shuntei (?~1824)

八四

本村　は、棒の達人として斯界に名を馳せた人である。彼は文武の偉丈夫の典型ともいひ得べく、六尺棒を押ッ執つて敵に向ふ如き、四邊に人なきが如くであつた。その一例に彼は室の兩壁に僅かに棒が遣入るほどの穴を穿ち自分は室の中央に立つて棒を左右に振り立て、件の穴の中に差し込んで、百發百中、一囘たりとも誤つことがなかつたさうである。

崎原と外間　は、二人同時代の人で、共に強力無双の人として知られてゐる、殊に外間は松村と共に、薩摩の人伊集院氏より劍道の指南をうけ「打ち込み」の達人であつた。

宇久田と松元　は、突手として知られてゐる。

太田按司は、弟長小樽と共に、強力の所持者としてのみならず、智勇兼備の武人であつた。

赤平の石嶺　も、強力の持主であつた。

この外にも、當時の武士としてその名を知られてゐる人に、油屋山城　は、餘り世人には知られないけれども、態々支那に行つて、唐手の研究をなした程の人で弓にも長じてゐたといふ。

220

Martial Artists During the Era of:

Sho Sei 尚成王 (1800 ~ 1803) **Sho Ko** 尚灝王 (1787 ~ 1834)

Motomura was an expert at the Bo, the wooden staff, and the fame of his prowess spread to every area. He was the epitome of a man who was both strong and dependable. When he took hold of his Rokushaku Bo, 180 cm/ 5'9" wooden staff, even if he was surrounded by opponents on all four sides, it was like they weren't even there.

Another example of his training method was he bored two holes in the walls of his room, one on the front wall, one on the back. He would then stand in the center of the room and practice Bo Furi, spinning the Bo on his left side and right side. He would then suddenly stab the end of his Bo forward, so that it slid perfectly into one hole or the other. If he did this thrust a hundred times he would fit the end of his Bo in the holes a hundred times, without a single mistake.

Sakihara and **Hokama** were both alive at the same time and were both known for having unparalleled strength. Further, Hokama along with Matsumura studied Kendo under a man from Satsuma Domain named Ishuin and became a master of Uchi Komi, moving in and striking.

Ukuda and **Matsumoto** were well known for their skill in Tsukite 突手, striking.

Ota Anzu together with his younger brother Nagasutaruu were not only known for having great strength but also as warriors who were brave and wise.

Akahira of Sekirei (Ishimine) was also known for his great strength. In addition to the men mentioned above, there were also the following Bushi, warriors/ martial artists.

Andaya Yamagusuku was not well-known but he made a great effort to travel to China and study Karate there. He was also an expert archer.

松村●當間●野村 は、共に同時代の武人であつた。　松村先生は、人も知る壯勇無雙の人、氏は武氏、名は成逹、自ら壯勇と號し、足を自由に扱ひ、よく蹴り上げることに妙であつた。時に、同驛の人が背後から抱き止めて彼を武みんとした時、彼は手の自由を失び乍らも、自由に足を左右に蹴上げ、背後より抱き締めてゐる人を蹴倒したさうである。　松村は、亦劍客でもあつた。一說に依ると、彼は叔父某の仇を報ひる爲め、態々支那に行つて唐手を學び、且つ劍術の指南を藤原の有名な劍客伊集院氏より受け、其の奧儀を究めたといふ。

彼は武をよくしたのみならず、當時の秀才、書家としても一家をなし、文人墨をも克くした。三十歳の頃より、尚泰王の御側役であつた。王が御惡戲が好きで、管て勝牛と武令した事がある。

當時有名なる猛牛があつて、御別莊に飼はれてあつたが、先生は王の御惡戲を豫期して居たので、早速牛舍に行つて見たら案の狀猛牛は人を見たい、足を踏み鳴らし、鼻息荒く突掛つて來る。先生は最初の程拳骨で突てみたが中々弱らない、益々猛烈な勢ひで突て來るので、今度は持つてゐる扇子で突掛つて來る度にその目をなぐつたら、さすがの牛もへこたれて仕舞つた。先生はそれから傾日牛舍に行つて、それを繰り返された。

吾々は此處に武人の用意周到さを知ることが出來るであらう。即ち、先生は前以て牛の弱點を知り、亦牛に

八五

Matsumura, Toma and **Nomura** were all warriors from the same era.

Matsumura Sensei was known as a man of unparalleled bravery. He was born into a Samurai family and his name was Naritatsu. He gave himself the martial arts name of Unyu, cloud-brave. He was able to use his feet freely and had mastered the art of kicking with a Keri Age, Rising Kick. Once when a friend tried to grab him from behind and arrest his movement, Matsumura Sensei, who's arms were pinned, used both his legs to kick the person holding him from behind, knocking him down and thereby freeing himself.

He was also an expert swordsman. One story about him states that he travelled to China to learn Karate in order to avenge the murder of a certain uncle. He also received sword instruction from a master swordsman from Satsuma named Ishuin and he was eventually able to become enlightened to the inner mysteries of the way of the sword. Not only did he study martial arts but he was also a master calligrapher, starting his own school and producing many paintings in the Southern China style. At the age of twenty he entered the service of King Sho Ko as an attendant. The king was very fond of mischief and pranks and he once made Matsumura Sensei fight a bull.

The story goes: at the time there was a bull famous for its ferocity that was being raised at one of the King's villas. Matsumura Sensei had suspected the king might pull some sort of prank so when he arrived at the villa he immediately went to the bullpen. Just as he had been told, at the very sight of a human the bull became angry, pawing at the round with its hoofs and puffing fierce blasts of air out of its nose. Then it charged. At first Matsumura Sensei tried striking it in the nose with the bones of his fist, but the blows didn't seem to weaken the beast, and in fact seemed to increase its fury. So, the next time the bull charged Matsumura Sensei used his Sensu, folding fan, to strike the beast in the eye. This blow to a vital point staggered even the raging bull. For the next several days Matsumura Sensei went to the bullpen and repeated this duel. We, as martial artists, can see what he was preparing for. In other words Matsumura Sensei had discovered the bull's weak point and the bull, for its part, knew this as well and became frightened.

もそれを知らしめ、そして恐れしめたのである。

處が王は案の狀、闘牛との試合を先生に命ぜられ、先生はお受けした。愈々當日になつて闘牛場には柵をめぐらし觀衆は片唾を呑んで待つてゐる。例の猛牛は兩方より繩を付け引張られて登場した。先生はと見ればいつもの通りの服装で手に扇子を持つのみである。王は非常に氣づかはれて、身輕になる樣御沙汰があつたが、先生は平然としてづかづか栅の中に入り、扇子を以て身構へるのみ。試合は好何にと云へば、件の巨牛は三四度突掛つて來たが、其の都度先生の爲に目を突かれて恐れを爲し、先生が進めば、尻込みして逃げ廻るばかりである。觀衆は全く恐嘆し先生の許ばんが益々盛になつたそうであつた。先生はいつも、私達に武人の用意周到さ、如何に頭の働が必要であるかを説かれて居た。

序に、屋部憲通君は先生のお隣りであつたので、餘程先生から可愛がられて居た一人である。當間親雲上は、これ又松村時代の人で、力量衆に勝れ熱心たる唐手の研究家であつた。

野村は身の丈五尺五寸餘の巨漢で、體軀堂々一撃のもとに人を突き倒すのに妙を得て居たといふ、そして彼の一撃に堪へる者がなく、一代の拳骨武士として後世にその名を殘した。

As was expected the King ordered Matsumura Sensei to duel the bull and he agreed. Eventually the day of the duel came and all the people standing around the fence of the circular bullpen were holding their breath in anticipation. The fierce bull was led to the ring by two men pulling it with ropes. As for Matsumura Sensei he was dressed as he always was and held his folding fan in his hand.

The King watched anxiously as Matsumura Sensei casually walked unarmed into the fenced off area inside the bullpen and then stood waiting with just a folding fan in his hand. As for how the duel actually went, the bull started to charge three or four times however each time the beast became scared that Matsumura Sensei would strike him in the eye, so if Sensei advanced the bull would drop back and then scamper around the bullpen, avoiding his opponent. The spectators were thunderstruck by this and Matsumura Sensei found his reputation had risen considerably due to this victory.

Matsumura Sensei always talked about the importance of *Yoh-I Shu Toh*, being prepared, and realizing you will have to use your head.

Incidentally Yabu Kentsu was a neighbor of Matsumura Sensei who doted on him like a son.

Tohma Pe-chin who lived around the same time as Matsumura Sensei was blessed with great strength and he was passionate about Karate and trained extensively.

Nomura was a giant of a man standing 5 Shaku 5 Sun, 1.7 meters/ 5'5." It is said he had trained his body so that with one hit he could knock a man down. At the time there was not a single man who could withstand a single punch from Nomura. He was the Kenkotsu Bushi, Warrior of the Fist, of his age and his fame extended to the following generations.

大城と金城は、共に同時代の人である。大城は力量にすぐれ研究に餘念なく、金城は筋骨隆々、姿勢を正して拳骨を握る時、その堅きこと正に石の如きものがあつたと言ふ。

筑佐事儀間は、力量の點に於て、並ぶものなく、武人として後世の人に喧はれ針をよくしたと傳へられる

寒川の石嶺は、身輕で技が敏捷で、且つ傳統的唐手の保持者として知られて居る。

尚ほ近代の武人中智慧者佐久間は、井戸の中に飛び込み、兩股を張つて身を前間に支へ、水中に落ちることがなかつたといふ。亦蓆を身體に巻付け、只兩手と頭のみを出して一氣に四尺の溝の中を飛び出したとは苦心の程が偲はれる。

國頭は熱心なる研究家で技も早く多和田の足技も共に並び稱された。

喜屋武は有名な人で身體の固きこと金鐵の如きものがあつた。

豐見城・親方は、近代の武人で、糸洲翁と時代を等しくし、コイ流の名人でもあつた。其の愛弟子としては現に伊是名朝睦氏が存命中である。豐見城は亦鎗術にも長じてゐて、それは唐手以上といふ評があり、殊に、馬上に於ける鎗術が得意で、彼が六尺豐た栗毛の馬に股がつて槍を執る時、如何なる強敵も尻込みしたさう

八七

Ou Gusuku and **Kin Gusuku** both lived in the same era. Ou Gusuku was a powerful man who trained relentlessly. Kin Gusuku had a straight stance and well-developed muscles. When he squeezed his hand into a fist, it felt as hard as stone.

Chikusa Jigima's strength was so great he was unparalleled while alive and later generations of martial artists sung songs about him. It is told that he was also trained the Sai extensively.

Ishirei from Sanyaa[15] was very light on his feet and his movements were deft and quick. He is also famous for preserving traditional Karate.

From a relatively recent period there was the martial artist and intellectual Sakuma. He was known for being able to jump in a well and stop himself from dropping into the water at the bottom by flexing his thighs against the walls of the well. He also wrapped his body in a grass mats that only his head and hands were exposed. The fact that with one burst of strength he was able to break through the 4 Shaku, 120 cm/ 3'11" long length of woven grass mat is testament to his severe training.

Kunjyan was a passionate practitioner whose fast technique was said to be equivalent to the Tawada kicking techniques.

Kiyan who was famous for having a body so hard it was like iron.

Toyomi Gusuku Oyakata is a fairly recent martial artist. He was active around roughly the same time as the revered gentleman Itosu. He was also a master of Koi Ryu. His favored student is Izena Chofuku who is still alive today. Toyomi Gusuku also excelled at Sojutsu, spear fighting, and in fact he was more regarded in that art than Karate. Toyomi was particularly skilled at wielding a spear while on horseback. He stood 6 Shaku, 180 cm/ 5'9" tall and when he mounted his chestnut colored horse and took up his spear, his foes were likely to lose their nerve and drop down on their butts when faced with this fearful opponent.

---

[15] Earlier this name was written as "Ishimine from Samukawa."

Translator's Note:

Illustration of Archery and Cannon Practice

Translator's Note:

Illustration of Archery and Cannon Practice

Initially they trained Kawasaki School Taiho, Cannon, and later followed the teachings of the elder Nanki. The islanders all still practice today.

- Various Tales from the Southern Isles (Ryukyu)
-By Nagoya Sagenta (1820~1881)

である。

豊見城と同時代の人に、玉城親方といふ人があつたが、彼は眞喜屋の高弟として師の寵愛を受け而も乗馬術の達人で、シントウ流をよくし、弓にも長じてゐた。此の二人は琉球に於ける馬術双壁とうたはれてゐる。

牧志は、縄切りの名人で、彼はよく縄で自分の身體を二重三重に巻き付け氣合もろとも縄を見事に切ることが出来た。亦白布の木綿で頭丈に頭に八巻をさせ、その八巻を頭を一振り振つて抜きとつたさうである。

安里・糸洲の兩翁は極く最近の首里の武人である。安里翁は身體が輕く技が素早く、糸洲翁は專ら研究的態度で終始し巻藁の稽古に熱心で近代の武人としては稀に見る突き手であつた。

右の兩氏より、やや後輩に屬するが突手として知られてゐる、首里の喜友名と板良敷の三翁がゐる。板良敷はアカー山として知られ、現在八十一歳の高齢であるが、元氣壮者をしのぐものがある。身軀偉大、馬術もよくし、唐手は洗練されたる技術の保持者である。亦氏は八重山節の名歌手でもある。

那覇に於ける武人には、首里の上原時代の具志が尤も有名で、敏捷なる卓業と突手で知られてゐる。

長濱は突手の名人で糸洲翁が師事した人である。

In the same era as Toyomi Gusuku, there was also a man named **Tama Gusuku Oyakata**. He was a high-level student of Makiya. Makiya Sensei was quite fond of Tama. Further, Tama was an expert at Bajutsu, the equestrian arts and was also a practitioner of Shinto Ryu. Further he also studied archery. These two men were praised as two pillars of the equestrian arts.[16]

Makishi was a Nawa Kiri no Tatsujin, an expert at escaping from ropes.[17] He would have two or three coils of rope tied around his body with a ferocious shoult and he would break free in a spectacular fashion. He would also tie a strip of white cotton cloth tightly around his head. With one great whip of his head he could send the cloth headband flying.

The two revered gentleman **Asato** and **Itosu** are from the generation immediately preceding the current one. They were both martial artists from Shuri.

The revered gentleman **Anri** was very light on his feet and executed his techniques quickly.The revered gentleman Itosu never wavered from his dedication to training. Throughout his life he continued to passionate about Makiwara training. Contemporary martial artists thought his Tsuki-te, way of striking, was remarkable.

Two revered gentleman of Shuri, **Kiyuna** and **Itaryoshiki** were could perhaps be considered Kohai, juniors, to the previously mentioned revered gentleman were well-known as Tsuki-te, striking.

Itaryoshiki was known as Aka-yama. At preset he is eighty-one years old but is a very energetic elder who still strives hard. He was blessed with a strong body and he practiced Bajutsu, equestrian arts, extensively. He is known for having refined and maintained an excellent Karate technique. He is also a famous singer of songs from the Yaeyama, Eight mountains area of Okinawa.

---

[16] The prase used is "two walls" but the meaning is "one cannot be said to be greater or lesser than the other."
[17] Though this has the word "cut" it doesn't necessarily mean breaking the rope itself, it can mean "escaping from being tied up."

桑江は、當時那覇に於て屋部氏と並稱された人で、身體の大きいこと金鐵のごとく頑丈な偉丈夫であった。

泊の武人中では、何といっても松茂良・親泊・山田の三者が抜群の譽を顯ち得てゐる。

松茂良は、突手の名人で自分（著者）も時々伺って教へを乞ふたが先生の教授法は、絶えず弟子に工夫させて居られた。琉球の唐手教授法は概してさうで、其風しない人々の技は、中々進歩しない、只々身體を鍛くするのみである。

親泊は、足技の達人であった。

山田に至っては身體を鬪くするといふ特技の持主で、桑江氏と共に、この稀で並稱されてゐる。

その他糸洲時代の久米村の武人、村山は力量象に秀で、稀代の壯漢であった。

最期に、城間村の棒古波藏と古波藏村の宮平を紹介して、この稿を終るが、昔より琉球の武人は、唐手のみで終始せず、何れも特技を有してゐた。この二房者も、功棒と乗馬術に秀で、古波藏は松村時代の棒者とし

て一二を爭った。

宮平も、同時代の武人として相當名を知れ亦乗馬術の達人として大に斯界に名を馳せ互蠻の持主であった。

八九

As for martial artists in Naha, the most famous is probably **Gushi**, who lived in the same era as Uehara of Shuri. He was known for his swift and nimble execution of Waza and Tsuki-te, striking.

Nagahama is famous for his Tsuki-te. The elderly gentleman Itosu had Nagahama as a teacher.

At that time in Naha, **Kuwae** was considered equivalent to Nagahama. His body was solid and felt like it was forged of iron. Truly a paragon of physical strength.

As for the martial artists in Tomari are concerned, three names stand out: Matsumura, Oyadomari and Yamada. These three can definitely be considered the cream of the crop.

Matsumura was well-known for his Tsuki-te, striking. I (the author) sometimes went and paid my respects in order to receive training from him. He taught his students to develop new Kufu, tricks of the trade or workarounds, when training Karate. Generally speaking this aspect of Karate instruction is paramount in Ryukyu. Those that don't develop Kufu never really seem to advance and they are only able to make their bodies more rigid.[18]

Oyadomari was an expert at Ashiwaza, leg techniques.

Yamada had a particular method to harden the body. In this respect he was equivalent to Kuwae.

Among the other martial artists active during the Itosu era in Kume Village, there was **Yamamura** who was head and shoulders above all the other strong men in terms of power.

---

[18] Motobu Choki uses two different Kanji combinations to refer to Kufu 工夫 and 具風. The word Kufu refers to tricks of the trade or a knack that is used by both craftsmen, artists and martial artists. In martial arts it is frequently seen when you isolate one aspect of a Kata and train that in a certain way before re-incorporating it into the Kata.

Lastly, I would like to introduce **Bo Kohagura** of Kusukuma Village as well as **Miyadaira** of Kohagura Village. Though this will end the section of my book discussing martial artists in old Ryukyu, understand that they did not study Karate alone, but each had a specialty. Both of these men excelled at Bo, the wooden staff, and Joba Jutsu, equestrian art. During the Matsumura era, Miyadaira was invariably either the number one or number two ranked wooden staff practitioner.[19]

As for Miyadaira he was well-known amongst the martial artists of his era. In particular he was renowned as an expert at Joba, horse riding, as well as for being a giant of a man.

---

[19] The Kanji for Bo Kohagura's first name is Bo 棒 "wooden staff" and he excelled at the wooden staff, so maybe it is a nickname. His last name is Kohagura 古波蔵 "old wave storehouse" which is the name of the village where Miyadaira is from.

Joba Jutsu is a more contemporary term for Bajutsu. Both mean "equestrian arts" however Bajutsu implies using horses in war while Joba is more horseback riding in general.

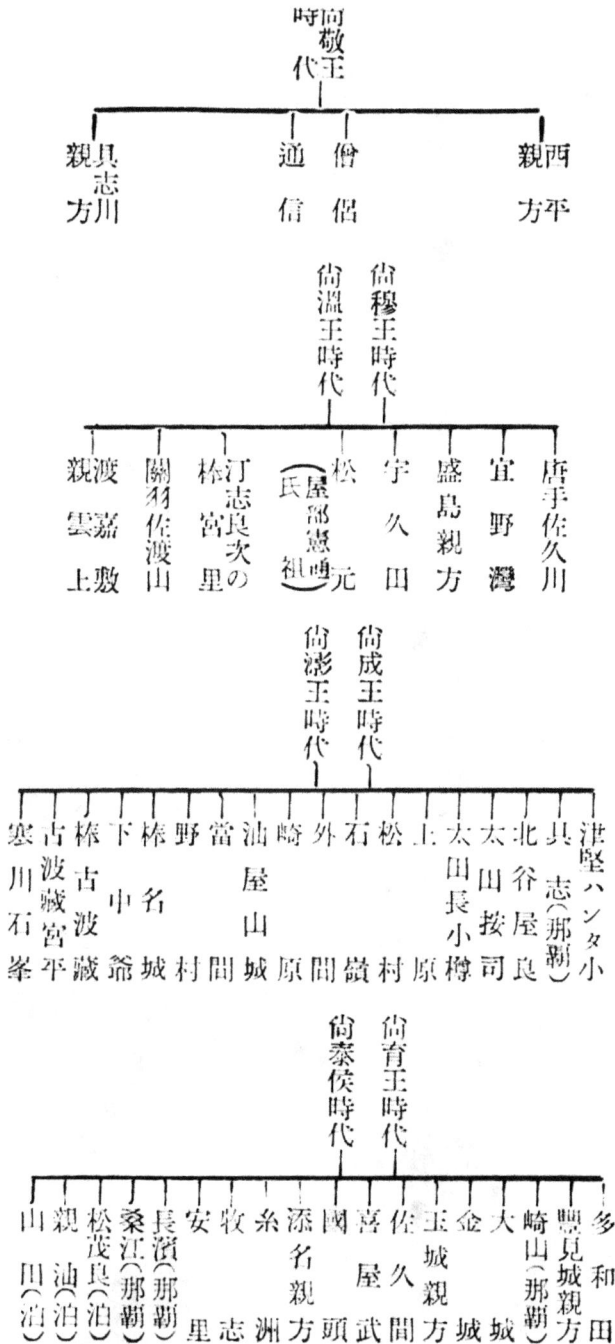

向敬王時代

- 具志川親方
- 僧侶
- 道信
- 西平親方

尚穆王時代　尚温王時代

- 唐手佐久川
- 宜野灣
- 盛島親方
- 宇久田
- 松元
- 屋部憲通（氏祖）
- 汀志良次の栋宮里
- 關羽佐渡山
- 親雲上渡嘉敷

尚成王時代　尚灝王時代

- 港堅ハンタ小
- 具志（那覇）
- 北谷屋良
- 太山按司
- 太田長小樽
- 上原
- 松村
- 石嶺
- 外間
- 崎城
- 油屋
- 富名腰
- 野村
- 棒屋良山
- 下名城
- 棒古波蔵爺平
- 古波蔵宮平
- 寒川石峯

尚育王時代　尚泰侯時代

- 多和田
- 崎山（那覇）
- 豊見城親方
- 大城
- 金城
- 玉城親方
- 佐久間
- 喜屋武
- 國頭
- 添石洲
- 糸名里
- 牧志
- 安村
- 長濱（那覇）
- 桑江（那覇）
- 松茂良（泊）
- 親油（泊）
- 山田（泊）

Martial Artists During the Era of:

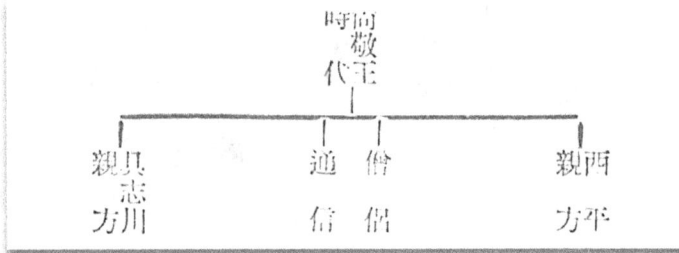

King Sho Kei 尚敬王 (1700 ~ 1752)

Nishida Oyakata
The Monk Tsushin
Gushirawa Oyakata

Martial Artists During the Era of:

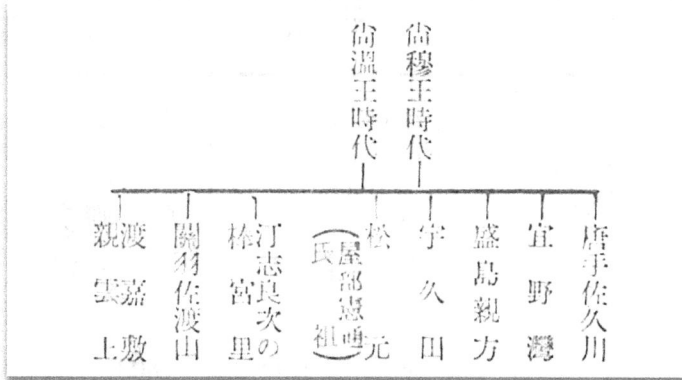

尚穆王時代　尚温王時代

唐手佐久川　宜野灣　盛島親方　宇久田　松茂良（屋部恩元）祖恩　汀志真次の宮里　栂宮次の宮里　闕羽佐渡山　親雲上渡嘉敷

King Shō Boku 尚穆王 (1739 ~ 1794)
King Shō On 尚温王 (1784 ~ 1802)

Karate Sakugawa
Ginowan Donchi
Morishima Oyakata/ Makabe Chaanga
Ukuda
Matsumoto (the forefather of Yabu Kentsu 1866 ~ 1937)
Bo Miyazato from Choshiraji
Kanu Sadoyama
Tokashiki Pe-chin

Martial Artists During the Era of:

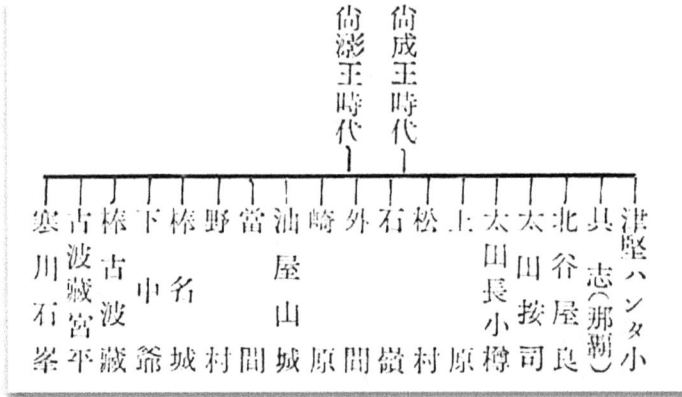

尚澎王時代　尚成王時代

寒川石峯　古波藏宮平　棒古波藏　下小城　棒名村　野間　富城　油間　崎山城　外間　石嶺　松原　上村　太田長小橙　太田按司　北谷屋良　具志（那覇）小　津堅ハンタ小

King Shō Sei 尚成王 (1800 ~ 1803)
King Shō Kō 尚灝王 (1787 ~ 1834)

Tsuken Hantaga
Chantan Yara, Ota Ansu
Ota No Nagasutaru-
Uehara, Matsumura
Ishimine from Akahira
Hokama, Motomura
Sakihara
Andaya Yamagusuku
Toma Pe-chin
Nomura
Bonagusuku
Shichanakausunme-
Ishimine from Sunga-
Ohgusuku, Kanagusuku,

Martial Artists During the Era of:

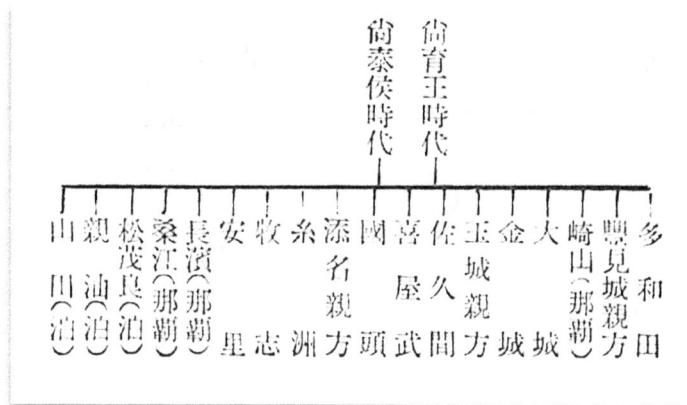

尚泰侯時代　尚育王時代

多和田　豐見城親方　崎山（那覇）　大城　金城　玉城親方　佐久間　喜屋武　国頭　添石　糸洲　牧志　安里　長濱（那覇）　桑江（那覇）　松茂良（泊）　親雲上（泊）　山田（泊）

King Shō Iku 尚育王 (1813 ~ 1847)
King Shō Tai 尚泰王 (1843 ~ 1901)

Tawada
Toyomigusuku Oyakata
Sakiyama (from Naha)
O-gusuku
Kana-gusuku
Tamashiro Oyakata
Sakuma
Kyan
Kunjan
Suishi Oyakata
Itosu
Makishi
Asato
Nagahama (from Naha)
Kuwae (from Naha)
Matsumura (from Tomari)
Yamada (from Tomari)

Translator's Note: Other Martial arts practiced by the Karate practitioners mentioned by Motobu Choki.

剣術 Kenjutsu (Sword Arts, including wooden sword)	Gushikawa Oyakata Hokama Matsumura
槍術 Sojutsu (Spear Arts)	Nishihira Oyakata Kanu Sadoyama Motomura Toyomi Gusuku Oyakata
弓術 Kyujutsu (Archery)	Tama Gusuku Oyakata Bo Kohagura KanKohagura
棒術 Bojutsu (Wooden Staff)	Tsuken Hantaga Shikyanaka Usumii Giwan Donchi Miyadaira Itoman Magii Bo Kohagura
釵術 Sai Jutsu (Sai Techniques)	Uehara Chikusa Jigima
馬術・乗馬 Bajutsu (Equestrian Arts)	Toyomi Gusuku Oyakata Tama Gusuku Oyakata Bo Kohagura Miyadaira
相撲 Sumo (Wrestling)	Toyomi Gusuku Toman Magii

近代武人の逸話
Kindai Bujin no Itsuwa
Anecdotes Regarding
Contemporary Martial Artists

近代武人の逸話

斯界の麒麟兒具志川思龜武勇傳

世に佐部の親方として、後世に名を殘した西平親方の高弟に赤平の人具志川思龜がある。彼は、もと猫地家の出にして、兄は雲巖といひ、琉球の名僧としてよく知られてゐる。而して彼も亦鬼をも拉ひじぐやうな武談逸話の持主として知られ、名を後世に殘した。當時、琉球政府に於ては若衆といふ職制があり、其の頃年齡僅かに十三歳の彼は、若衆として城勤めをなしてゐたのであるが、或る日、思龜が同じ若衆の友達三名と打ち連れて城内よりの歸途さ、タマ〲阿旦川の前を通りかかつた所、餘りに咽喉が渇き、水が欲しくなつたので川の邊に汲みおいた桶の水を無斷に飲み干したのである。所が最前より此の有様を凝視てゐた中田殿内の下男某は、烈火の如く憤ほり、強力無双をもつて恐れられてゐるのを鼻にかけ思龜の襟首を捕へ、誇るのも諾かず傍若無人の振舞ひを敢てし、猶も太い拳骨を彼の頭上に見舞つた。流石の彼も泣きながら家に逃げ歸り、その由を父親方に物

Anecdotes Regarding Contemporary Martial Artists
Heroic Tales of Gushikawa Umikami the Martial Arts Prodigy

There was once a person from Akahira named Gushikawa Umikami whose name is remembered by posterity. He was the leading disciple of Nishidaira Oyakata who was also known as Sabi no Oyakata. Umikami was born into the Haneji household. His older brother, Ungan "Cloud above the Rock" was a priest known throughout Ryukyu. His name is still famous today due to the many stories about Umigami's martial arts prowess that seem to recall children's stories of boys besting devils.

At that time, there was a position in the Ryukyu Government called Wakashu, young advisor. When Umikami was just thirteen years old, he began serving at Shuri Castle as a Wakashu. One day Umikami along with two or three friends who held the same position, decided to travel home from the castle together.

They happened to pass by Atan River along the way home and Umikami realized he was deathly thirsty. Seeing a wooden bucket full of water near the river, he drank all of it without permission.

However, it turns out a certain servant of Nakata Donchi[20], who had been watching the situation while glowering, exploded in rage, terrifying the group with his unparalleled strength. The servant seized Umikami by the back of his collar and, despite the boy's apologies, cracked him on the head with his massive fist.

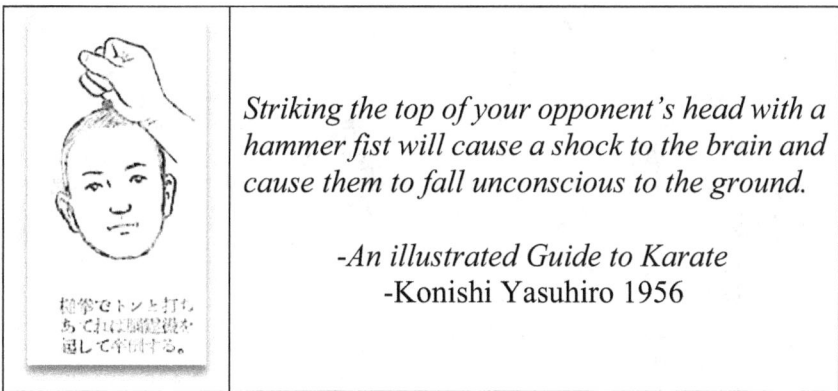

Striking the top of your opponent's head with a hammer fist will cause a shock to the brain and cause them to fall unconscious to the ground.

-An illustrated Guide to Karate
-Konishi Yasuhiro 1956

---

[20] A Donchi 殿内 "Inner Lord" is a rank in the Ryukyu Kingdom referring to a Samurai who manages an area of land.

語つた。それから彼は彼の下男よりうけた恥辱を是非雪がんものと、涙ながらに父親方に乞ひ、當時天下に名を馳せてゐた佐部の親方に懇願して弟子となつたのである。尤も佐部の親方は思凱を一見せられただけで、

「こは將來、琉球随一の武人となり、後世に屹度名をなすであらう」と觀破せられ、父親方より萬事を引きうけ、自ら手にとつて唐手の指南をされた。其後數年ならずして思凱は一角の武人となり、十六の時からは師匠佐部の親方の高弟として許されたが、些しも奢りたかぶることもなく、常に謙讓の態度で人に接し、斯界の麒麟兒として高名をほしいま〳〵にしたといふ。

殊に、彼が沈勇たりしことは、之亦色々の口碑として後世に傳へられてゐるが、其の一二を舉ぐれば、或る時佐部の親方が彼の武人としての注意力を試さんとせられ、敷居越しに彼の名を呼んだ所、彼は平然として敷居の所に三指をつきて膝まづき、手にせる扇子をもつて敷居の溝におき、以て襖を閉められた時の用心にした。師匠佐部の親方は之を見て僅か十六才の彼が斯程までに物事に注意深く、且つ武士としての沈着を常に忘れない態度を激賞されたそうである。

尚ほ、彼れが十七才の折、嘗つて阿豆川に於て彼の強力無双の下男よりうけた恥辱

After this thrashing Umikami fled home in tears and told the story to his father. He begged his father to find a way for him to rid himself of the shame he incurred at the hands of the servant. So, Umikami became the student of Sabi no Oyakata, who was the greatest martial artist under the heavens at the time.

As it turns out, Sabi no Oyakata, taking one look at Umikami, could see through to the boy's true nature and remarked,

In the future, he will become the greatest martial artist in Ryukyu. This boy's name will be remembered for generations.

Sabi no Oyakata took full responsibility for the boy from the father and instructed Umikami personally in Karate. Within a few years, Umikami became martial artist who was a cut above the rest. At the age of sixteen Sabi no Oyakata promoted Umikami to the rank of top disciple. Despite this Umikami was not arrogant and treated other people with respect and humility. He became renowned as a Young Kirin, a child prodigy.

There are several oral traditions that describe his Chinyu, calm bravery, that have been handed down through the generations and I would like to share one or two of them here.

One day, Sabi no Oyakata, wanting to test Umikami's attentiveness as a warrior, called out to him from his study. Responding in a typical fashion, Umikami knelt at the entrance to the study and bowed, placing the first three fingers of each hand on the ground. As he did this he placed the folding fan he was holding in his hand into the groove at the bottom of the sliding door to prevent it from being shut. Upon seeing a boy of only sixteen be in possession of such a level of adherence to everyday caution, he praised the lad highly for his martial mentality.

度を激賞されたそうである。尚ほ、彼れが十七才の折、嘗つて阿豆川に於て彼の強力無双の下男よりうけた恥辱

を雪ぐべく御前試合を師を介して言上した。愈々両三日の中に平良馬場に於て真剣勝負を決するといふ或る日の

こと彼は高鼾をかいて四畳半の自分の座敷に午睡をしてゐた。 折りしも師佐部の親方は思龜の許に訪ねられ、

座敷におけるかの豪膽なる寝態を見られ、父親方の面前で六尺棒をしごいて打つてかゝられた。 處が寝てゐた

儘の彼はガバと跳ね起き、あたりに積み重ねてあつた疊を以て師匠から打ち込まれた棒を受け流し、以て平然た

りしといふ。

斯くて彼は僮々数年の中に佐部の親方の薫育を受けて琉球随一の武人となり、平良馬場の御前試合に於て、見

事彼の強力無双の下男を一撃のもとに打ち倒し、後世にその名を馳せたのである。

Further, once after Umikami had turned seventeen he sought to erase the shame he had received when he had been thrashed by the servant of unparalleled strength at Adan River. Umikami requested that Sabi no Oyakata submit a formal challenge for a duel in front of the King. The Shinken Shobu, fight to the death, would be held within three days at the Taira equestrian training ground.

One day Umikami was snoring loudly while taking a nap in his four and a half tatami mat room. As it happened his teacher Sabi no Yakata had come by for a visit. Seeing Umikami sprawled out sleeping Sabi grabbed a Rokushaku Bo and, in front of Umikami's father, swung the wooden staff at the boy. Despite the fact that Umikami was apparently sound asleep, he leapt up and calmly seized one of the extra Tatami mats that were stacked nearby and blocked his master instructor's attack with a Uke Nagashi, block that passes the energy of the attack to the side. This was all done calmly.

Thus due to being immersed in Sabi no Oyakata's training, within a few years Umikami had become the premier martial artist in Ryukyu.

Regarding the duel at Taira equestrian ground, which would be in front of the King, Umikami knocked the servant of unparalleled strength to the ground with one blow, causing the name Umikami to reverberate for generations.

Sumo
From: *Illustrations of Ryukyu Traditions and Culture*
Edo Era

Toyomi Gusuku Who Won a Local Sumo Tournament

Toyomi Gusuku was a man famed as a practitioner of Goi Ryu Bajutsu, Goi School equestrian arts, in addition to being an expert at Sojutsu, Spear fighting.[21] There is also an impressive tale of how he entered and won a Sumo match that was taking place out in the countryside.

This occurred just at the time he had turned twenty-four years old. One day in the summer he was riding his beloved horse between the villages of Katsuhara and Haebaru when he came across a local Sumo tournament taking place on an equestrian training ground. In the ring was a rough fellow who had won several matches in a row. Every time a new challenger emerged the rough fellow would throw them to the ground. Some of the challenges were even forced to eat sand from the top of the earthen Dohyo Sumo mound. The young men in attendance were completely dejected by this humiliation and had begun to withdraw.

Seeing how the young people were being thrown around, the naturally chivalrous Toyomi immediately dismounted, his horse, yanked off his Kimono and Hakama and then threw them aside. He mounted the Dohyo mound to face the proud youth who had heretofore racked up one victory after another. Toyomi Gusuku defeated the man with a brilliant throw, and forced him to eat the sand of the Dohyo.

---

[21] Earlier in this book Motobu Choki refers to a Koi school of equestrian arts. Neither name appears in the *Bugei Ryuha Jiten*, encyclopedia of martial arts schools.

かくれたる棒の達人糸滿マギー

武人といふよりは、單に棒の達人として世に知られたる近世の朴訥漢糸滿マギーにも亦面白いエピソードがある。彼は今から約百五十年前の人で、糸滿で呱々の聲をあげ、池の端小のマギーと稱されて、世人からその名を唄はれてゐた。由來、糸滿は琉球唯一の漁村として知られ、村民は男女を問はず、擧って漁業にたづさはるのであるが、彼は幼い時から漁業を嫌ひ、朝から晩迄隣り近所の子供を相手に棒切れを振り廻し、大いに腕白子附振を

Itoman Magii: The Man Who Was Secretly a Master of the Wooden Staff

These days Toman Magii, who is described as Bokutotsukan, a rugged man, who is known today more for his expertise with the wooden staff rather than being a martial artist. This is an interesting episode about the man.[22]

He lived about 150 years ago and gave his first cries as a baby in Itoman village. His nickname was Ichi no Niiga-no Magii, Magii From the Edge of the Pond, and many people told stores of him.

Originally Itoman was known as the biggest fishing village in the Ryukyu Kingdom. In that village everyone, man or woman, worked in the fishing industry. However even as a child Magii despised fishing and instead he took up a Bo-kire, scrap of wooden pole and, from dawn to dusk, passed the time challenging the other local children to duels. He was a rather mischievous boy.

---

[22] Motobu Choki uses the English word episode エピソード written in the Katakana alphabet.

Translator's Note: Swords and Other Weapons in Ryukyu

Illustrations of Ryukyu Traditions and Culture
Edo Era

Kataki-uchi Revenge Killing
A martial arts demonstration recreating a famous revenge killing
with swords and Naginata, halberds.

Translator's Note: Swords and Other Weapons in Ryukyu

Illustrations of Ryukyu Traditions and Culture
Edo Era

Kataki-uchi Revenge Killing
A martial arts demonstration recreating a famous revenge killing
with swords and Naginata, halberds.
The two prisoners are bound with rope.

九六

發揮してゐた。後、成長して身の丈六尺一寸、體重實に二百有餘貫の偉丈夫となり、幼い時からの惡戯が役に立つて、二十才位には早や一角の棒者として斯界の人々から知られてゐた。殊に角力に鎧つては、古今獨歩と稱せられ、琉球角力界に於て、輾然と頭角を現はし、百五十年來彼と並ぶ者がなかつたのである。強て近代の力士中より、彼の面目に彷彿する力士を求むれば、先づ西原村伊保の濱の米須氏位で、僅かに其の面影を求め得るに過ぎないと思ふ。

斯く思ひ浮べる時、當時彼の眞價を考證すべき一挿話がある。それは或る時、首里の體見城親方と、那覇の崎山とが、共に連れ立つて彼を訪れ、其の腕前を試みとしたことである。崎山が彼に棒の試合を申込んだ所、彼は怪訝な顔をして「失禮では御座るが、貴男方は、お見掛けした處、未だお年も若い。私と立ち合ふなぞとは以ての外である。それに私の棒は、世間にこそ餘り知れてゐないが、自慢の角力歴以上に人一倍の苦勞をしたもので、自分では一角の棒者のつもりでゐる。况その上、體重の上でも、貴男方とは十斤二十斤の違ひなら未だしも八九十斤も隔つてゐる。如何してお相手なぞ出來ませう。お斷りになって、尚ほ一層懸命に武を練られた方が將來のお爲めで御座る。昔から、

Later he grew to be a large powerful man standing 6 Shaku 1 Sun and weighed 200 Kan.[23] As it turned out the mischief he had got up to as a youth was beneficial and by the time he had turned twenty he was the premier Bo staff practitioner in Ryukyu.

With regards to Sumo, he had a heretofore unheard of level of skill that put him on another plateau than the other wrestlers at the time. Such was his success that 150 years later he still has no equal. Among the Rikishi, Sumo wrestlers, of this day, if you were to ask who has any memories that could help flesh out Itoman Magii's character, you should first seek out Mr. Komesu of Iho Bay in Nishibara Village, though there are only the smallest vestiges of memories that remain.

The following story is one that Mr. Komesu recalled one time and it can serve as historical evidence regarding Itoman Magii.

One time, two men, Tomigusuku Oyakata of Shuri and Sakiyama of Naha set off together to visit Itoman Magii, seeking to test their skills against his. Sakiyama requested a wooden staff duel however, Magii looked rather dubious and replied, "This might sound a bit rude however after looking you over I have to say you seem quite young. Having a duel with you would be rather absurd. Though I am quite proud of my Sumo abilities, I have worked harder than anyone else to develop my skill with the Bo staff. Thus I feel I have carved out a niche for myself as a Bosha, or wooden staff practitioner."

Magii continued, "In addition, consider the weight difference between us. If you, young fellow, were only about ten or twenty Kin, 6~12 Kilograms/ 13~26 pounds, lighter than me that wouldn't make any difference, but there is an eighty or ninety Kin, 48~54 kilogram/ 63~71 pounds, weight difference between us. No matter how you look at it, you wouldn't stand a chance. Go home and dedicate yourself to forge your martial arts with all your ability."

[23] 1 Kan is about 3.8 kilograms/8 pounds, so 200 Kan would be 750 Kilograms/ 1653 pounds. It seems likely the author meant to use the unit of weight Kin, which is 0.6 kilograms/1.3 pounds meaning Magii weighed a respectable 120 kilograms/ 265 pounds.

「歌者は聲也、武者は力也」といふ諺も御座るから、よく〱稽古を勵まれ、あつぱれ琉球一の若武士とな

つて下さい。惡いことは申上げません。私みた様な年人は相手になさらず……又相手になつて立合つた所で決し

て貴男方の名譽となることは少しも御座いません。却つて今までのお名譽にキズつけるものと申しませう……。」

ときつぱり斷はつた。然し崎山の懇望いなみ難く、彼も一二合立合つた處、呵々大笑、

「最前も申上げた通り、失禮では御座るが、貴男方のお腕前では未だ〱私には及びません。更に武を練つて

後日、又お出でになつた方がよろしう御座います。更に相手になることがなかつた。彼マギーと懇見城との體重

の相違六十斤、崎山とは九十斤にも及び、彼マギーにとつては、全く問題にならなかつたのである。遺憾朦の間

見城親方も呆然として、二人は只彼の技術を時宮しスタコラ〱首里に錯つたのは正に珍中の珍談である。

私の唐手術 終

Magii concluded,

"From days long past there is an expression that goes,

For singers, the volume of their voice is the most important, for warriors it is the volume of their strength.

Thus you should be focusing all your efforts on training so that you become the most praiseworthy young warrior of Ryukyu. I do not have anything bad to say about you. A person of my age is not an appropriate opponent for you. Further, even if I were to agree to a duel with you would not emerge from it with even a small increase in prestige. In addition, such a duel might blemish the honor of your name that you have built up until now...."

And with that Magii decisively rejected the man's request for a duel.

On the other hand, Magii had a hard time refusing Tomigusuku's[24] request and the pair ended up facing off one or two times. However Magii stopped the fight mid-duel and, with a great laugh, said, "As I said before, and this may seem a bit rude, but your abilities are not developed enough to compete with me. I think you should focus on forging your abilities for a time and then consider issuing a challenge at a later time."

Thus Tomigusuku also did not meet with much success.

The difference in weight between Magii and Tomigusuku was about sixty Kin, 36 kilograms/ 79 pounds. So, even though Tomigusuku weighed close to ninety Kin, 54 kilograms/119 pounds, Magii had no trouble defeating him. Tomigusuku who prided himself on being a brave and powerful man was left thunderstruck by his defeat. Having seen the extent of Magii's skill Sakiyama and Tomigusuku could only shake their heads in amazement and slink back to Shuri.

Amongst the many amazing stories of such martial artists, this one truly stands out.

My Karate Jutsu
End

---

[24] The text actually says "Sakiyama" but this is probably referring to Tomigusuku as his name is mentioned at the end of this section.

著 者 略 歴

本部朝基翁は、幼名を三郎、緯名をサールー（猿）と稱す。明治三年四月五日、沖繩縣首里市赤平村本部按司の三男に生る。

幼にして武を好み、十二歳の時より長兄朝勇氏と共に糸洲翁を其の宅に聘し、正式に唐手の稽古を爲す。長ずるに及び、更に佐久間、松村の二翁に師事し、尚ほ組手に至りては右三氏の外、松茂良其他當時斯界に名ある武人は總て之を訪ねて教へを乞ひ、或は實地に立合ひ、專ら斯界の研究に沒頭す。當時の氏は、「武是れ我れ、我れ是れ武」の外に他念なく、從つて其の修業振りも到底常人の企及し得ざる處にして、寒中と雖も、夜具を用ひず、若し、それ寒さを覺ゆれば起きて型の稽古を爲し、暖まれば床に就くといふ有樣、或は亦組手に關する疑問あれば、寢食を忘れて工夫し、悟れば直に師を訪ねて實地に立合ひ、困難辛苦、以て其の練磨を怠らざりしと云ふ。

宜なるかな、二十四五の氏は既に武名赫々として、サールーと言へば誰知らぬ者もなく、人をして三舍を避けしむ。氏は今や齡老境に入る。而も尚豐鑠として子弟の養育に從事せらる。

余は、極めて、最近の知友に過ぎずと雖も、謙讓にして恬憺なる益々敬愛措くあたはざらしむるものがある。若し、それ技藝の點に至りては、既に世人の熟知せる處、敢へて吾人の贅言を用せざるべし。

（漢那朝常）

A Brief Outline of The Author's Life
By Kanna Chojo

Since the revered gentleman Motobu Choki was the third child in his family he was known as Saburo 三郎 "third son" as a youth. He also had the nickname *Saaruu*, which is the Okinawan way of pronouncing the Japanese word for "monkey" which is *Saru* 猿. He was born April 5th, 1870 as the third son of Motobu Anji in the Akihara section of Shuri, Okinawa Prefecture.

From a young age he liked martial arts and, at the age of twelve, started formal Karate training, along with his older brother Choyu, under the tutelage of the revered gentleman Itosu, who visited the Motobu house. He continued training over the years, eventually receiving further instruction from the revered gentlemen Sakuma and Matsumura.

With regards to Kumite, paired training, in addition to the three teachers mentioned above, Motobu Choki also visited Matsumora and many other contemporary Bujin, martial arts masters, and asked them for instruction. He also fought in many duels in the street. All in all he completely immersed himself in the pursuit of this art.

At the time, Motobu Choki's philosophy was solely, *If it is martial arts it is for me, if it is for me, it is martial arts*. Thus the amount of time he devoted to training went far beyond what most people would do. Even in winter, he would forgo blankets and endure the cold. When the cold eventually woke him, he would practice Kata. Once warm he would go back to bed. If he was having trouble figuring out some aspect of Kumite, he would forgo both food and sleep, until he had develop a Kufu, method of dealing with the problem. Once having become enlightened to the solution he would visit his teacher and practice it in a duel. A difficult and painful method of training. It is said that he was never negligent in his training.

By the age of twenty-four or five, he was already a renowned martial artist and you could not find a person that hand never heard of Saaruu, and people would keep their distance from him due to his fearful superiority.

Nowadays, though he is entering his later years, he is still a vigorous old man and devoted to educating his young disciples in

Karate.[25]

For my part, though I am only a fairly recent acquaintance, I am continually surprised not only by his modesty and unselfish manner but how he is always respectful of others. As far as his level of skill is concerned, since he is already known all over the world, anything I say here would be redundant.

---

[25] The "vigorous old man" is Kaku-shaku 矍鑠 in Japanese. The term originates from the *Tale of Ma Yuan* 馬援伝 contained within the *Book of the Later Han Dynasty* (5th century AD.)
The story is as follows:

During the reign of Emperor Guangwu, a rebellion broke out in the south. A general named Ma Yuan (14 BC ~ 49 AD) volunteered to ride south and put down the rebellion. However, the Emperor felt that since Ma Yuan was over sixty years old, he did not have the stamina. In response Ma Yuan mounted his horse and posed as if glaring at a target. The emperor laughed and said, "Hale and hearty, isn't he?" From then on the word Kaku-shaku was used to describe a person who is vigorous even in old age.

Ma Yuan is also famous for extolling his men to be committed to, "wrapping your body with horse leather" 馬革裹屍 which refers to being so dedicated to your responsibilities that you are willing to die on the battlefield and have your body be wrapped in horse leather.

Translator's Note

Kanna Chojo	Motobu Choki
Tsuruta Ryokan, Tokyo Manager Okinawa Food Company Director Born in Shuri	Karate Shihan (Head Instructor) Commonly known by the nickname Saaru. Born in Shuri
沖縄県人物風景写真大観 *Photographs of People and Places in Okinawa Prefecture* 1935	

昭和七年三月十日印刷
昭和七年三月十七日發行

著作者　本部朝基
東京市本鄉區臺町二番地

發行兼印刷者　漢那朝常
東京市神田區表猿樂町一九

印刷所　藤本印刷所
東京市本鄉區臺町二番地

發行所
東京市本鄉區臺町二番地
東京唐手普及會

Printed March 10th, Showa 7 (1932)
Published March 17th, Showa 7 (1932)

Author: Motobu Choki
Hongo Ward, Daimachi 2, Tokyo City

Printer and Publisher: Kanna Chojo
Kanda Ward, Omote Sarugaku Town, Tokyo City

Printer: Fujimoto Printers
Hongo Ward, Daimachi 2, Tokyo City

Publishing House: Tokyo Karate Fukyukai
(Tokyo Karate Promulgation Society)

本部朝基・MOTOBU CHOKI

Articles by or Related to Motobu Choki

本部朝基・MOTOBU CHOKI

キング
King Magazine
September 1925

『何んでもありませんが、あんな試合なら、私にも出來さうです。飛入りでやらして下さい』

『やらせろ！やらせろ！やらして下さい！』云つたのは監督の背後に先程から問答を聞いてゐた連中、氣紛れな爺さんが飛出して來たなと云はんばかりに。

『たまに飛入りをやらせるのも一興だ、第一人氣が立つ、やらせたがいゝ』

『でも君、柔道でもない、拳鬪でもないと云ふんだ、まさか田舎力士ぢやあるまいネ』

と、監督は、妙な笑ひを浮べながら、仲間に囁やいた。

『ま、ア、何んでもいゝさ、飛入りしたいと云ふからには、氣狂

ひでない限り、多少武術の心得はあるんだらう、やらせ給へ、やらせ給へ』

沖繩尚武會長　富名腰義珍氏

稀世の達人　本部朝基氏

唐手界の双璧

『さうか、よからう』

と監督は件の男に、

『では、演らせるとにします。が、規則は御承知なんでせうな、試合の規則は？』

『試合の規則？知りません』

『蹴り手と拳の突き手、打ち手は禁じられてゐるぜ』

『平手は？』

『無論構ひません、たゞ拳がいけないんです』

聞いて件の男は、微笑を浮べつゝ、

『やりませう』

とばかりノソく出て行きさうになつた。

『ア、モシ！』と監督は吃驚したやうに、

『やるはいゝが、何を着てやります、着物ぢや……』

『この儘で構ひません』

『その儘？』と遉がに並みゐる連中も呆氣にとられた。

『だつて、その儘ぢや剣が惡いネ、では、兎に角柔道衣を着て貰ひませう』

と監督は、飛んでもたいものが飛出して來たと云ふ面持で、用意の柔道衣を出した。

云はれるまゝに、件の男は、やをら、衣物を脱いで柔道衣に着換へたが、裸體になつて見ると驚いた、その全身の筋肉の

肉彈相搏つ
唐手拳鬪大試合

鳴絃樓主人

○不思議な田舎爺

大正十一年の秋十一月、京都市に催された衆鬪對柔道の大搏戰は、田にくゞくの嘲を生みつゝ、いやが上に讀都の人氣を煽り立てた。

「えらいもんやなう！　武德殿の試合は、毎年かゝさず見とるが、こんた猛烈な試合を見たとないう。まるで火の出るやうや！」

『方樣どすやろ、何せほんまに眞劒やさかい』などと、その日も場に溢れた觀衆は、とりぐの下馬評。その人氣に氣を得てか試合は各組とも愈々熱を加へ來たり、肉彈火花の大接戰、自然觀衆は、演者の一擊一投足にも、ハッ！　ハッ！　と膽を冷やしてゐた――その試合の眞最中、突然裝置屋へ訪づれたのは、見るから田舎爺らしい一人の男、

『飛入り試合をさして下さい』

『何？　飛入り？』

と、監督は、一寸意外な面持ちに出て來たが、

『貴下ですか、飛入りを申込んで來たのは？』

『さうです』

『して、その試合は、何誰がするんです？』

『私！』

と、監督は意外の面持に、少年がとり過ぎてゐる伜の男を、ヘンに思ひながら、斯うした試合をするには

『貴下、柔道家ですか？』

『いゝえ』

『では拳鬪でもおやりになつたんですか？』

『いゝえ』

『では何んですか？』

Nikudan Aiutsu
Two Unarmed Combatants Simultaneously Striking Each Other
Karate Kento O-Jiai
A Great Fight Between Karate and Boxing
By Meigen Roshujin

Fushigi na Inaka Oyaji
A Mysterious Old Man From the Countryside

In the autumn month of November in the eleventh year of the Taisho Emperor (1922,) a Boxing versus Judo tournament was held in Kyoto. The great bouts spurred many stories and rumors nearly every day and this only fanned the flames of excitement everyone in the city felt.

A Taisho Era ad for a Boxing vs Judo Tournament held in Osaka

Everyday inside the stadium was overflowing with speculation and rumor by the city folk, who said things like,

"It was amazing! I go to the Butokukai[26] tournament every year without fail, however I have never in my life seen such intense battles. They fought like they were on fire!"

"I agree, they were putting everything they had into those fights!"

The excitement carried over from one match to the next, only increasing in intensity. While watching these great duels of flesh striking flesh with an intensity that seemed to produce fireworks, the crowd began to naturally react to every strike, every throw and every kick with a Rah! Rah! of stunned surprise.

Suddenly, in the middle of one of the bouts, an older fellow who looked like he was from somewhere out in the countryside appeared at the stage door.

"*Tobi-iri Jiai wo Sashite Kudasai*? Can I enter the tournament at the last minute?"

"What? You want to just jump right in?" the man at the door replied.

The manager for his part had a dubious look on his face but asked,

"So you are looking to submit an application for someone to enter the tournament even though you didn't apply in advance?"

"That is correct" the country bumpkin said.

"So, who is the man who will be entering the tournament?"

"Me!"

"You?" the manager replied looking even more dubious than before, clearly thinking this man was a bit too old to be entering this sort of tournament. With a voice full of doubt he replied,

"Are you a Judo practitioner?"

"No"

"So then, you are a practitioner of the boxing arts?"

"No"

"So then, what do you do?"

"I don't do anything. That being said, I think I can handle myself in these types of bouts. Please let me enter last-minute."

[26] Dai Nippon Butoku Kai "Greater Japan Martial Virtue Society" was the largest martial arts organization in Japan. It was founded in Kyoto in 1895. The Butoku Kai held an annual tournament on May 4th featuring Kendo, Judo, Naginata and Kyudo competitions.

The two supporting walls of the Karate world
(right) President of Okinawa Shobu Funakoshi Gichin
(left) An Expert of Rare Ability Motobu Choki

Suddenly, from behind the manager a chant of, "Let him fight! Let him fight!" arose amongst the spectators that had heard the exchange between the old fellow from the country and the manager. Though the manager was just thinking he would turn the old fellow away since he was trying to enter a duel on the spur of the moment, but took a moment to think it over, "Well, it might be interesting to let a spur of the moment challenger enter the tournament. Most importantly the crowd will probably love it. Ok, It will be a good idea to let him fight."

The manager turned to the country bumpkin and said, "So then, you don't do Judo and you don't box, I hope you aren't going to try and use some Sumo that you learned out in the countryside?" The manager had said this with a wry grin on his face and turned to his friend and whispered, "Well, I suppose it doesn't really matter, anyone that would just want to jump into the ring like this must be a little crazy. He probably has some martial arts ability so I will let him have a go, I will let him fight."

"That sounds good." His friends replied.

Turning to the man in question the manager said,

"Very well, we will allow you to enter a bout, however you have to agree to the rules. Do you know the rules?"

"Rules for the bout? I have no idea."

"You can't use kicks, you can't strike with a closed fist and you can't chop with your hand."

"What about Hira-te, an open-handed strike?"

"It goes without saying that Hira-te is fine. However, you can't strike with a closed fist."

In response to this the old man from the countryside simply gave a small grin before quickly saying, "Then, let's us begin."

And with that he turned and began padding softly away.

"Just, just a moment!" the manager called out, stopping the man.

"We agreed that you would enter a bout, but what are you going to wear? Do you have a change of clothing?"

"I'm fine like this."

"You are going to fight wearing that?" the manager said as all those in hearing range gaped at the man.

The manager found his voice and said, "But won't it be difficult to fight in such clothing? Why don't I at least lend you a Judo uniform." With that, the manager, somewhat bewildered at this man who had appeared out of nowhere, found a Judo uniform and loaned it to the man. The man simply took the uniform and began undressing and changing into the Judo uniform.

However, when the man was undressed, everyone was shocked at what they saw. The older man from the country was absolutely rippling with muscles. In particular his arms had great bulges of muscles. For a man that appeared to be over fifty years of age, his body was the epitome of vigorous. Further, even more surprising was his waist. The lines of the muscles all around his waist and back seemed to be connected powerfully to his upper thighs. Even to the untrained eye the circumference of his waist was probably 4 Shaku 3 Sun, 130 centimeters/ 4'2"! Those in the backstage dressing room suddenly had an eerie feeling about this fellow.

"Who should we have him go up against? Seeing him with his clothes off made me realize he has a powerful body."

「チョージがいゝだら
う、あの男が本紙にな
つたら柔道なんか敵な
しだから」

「よからう」と、監督
は、例の男の名を訊い
て、早くも揭示板に
この組合せを貼り出
した。

『柔道家チョージ對、
飛入り、本部朝基』

○ピンアン四
段の構へ

「オイ、飛び入りが出
たぞ！」

『飛入り？』そいつは
愈々面白い！　成程

柔道家、チョージ對飛
入り本部朝基……チョ
ージ對飛入り本部朝基
……チョージといへば、こ
の拳闘家中の剛の者だが、相手は一體何物だらう？

飛入りだけは分つてゐるが、柔道家なのか何んだ
本部朝基？

「おほかた、
に觀客に

日本人だから柔道家なんだらう」

云つてゐる間もなく、やがて合圖と共に出て來た一方に、
に觀客に馴染のチョージ、長身肥大の名拳闘家だが、その相
手たる飛入り者は、と見れば、身長五尺四寸餘、肥滿しては
ゐ

如く、殊に節くれ立つた兩腕は、五十才以上に見える面貌とは似てもつかぬ逞しさ！隆起せる筋肉は、腰部と大腿部とをクッキリと割し、素人目にも、腰の周圍凡そ四尺三四寸とは、一目に分る！ 樂屋一同は、一寸薄氣味惡くなつて來た。

『誰れとやらせよう？裸體になつて見たら大變な身體をしてゐるぞ！』

『アッ！大事なとを忘れてゐた！本人は拳闘とやりたいのかな。それとも柔道と試合したいのかな？全く突然なんで、面喰つちやつた』

と監督は、またアクフタと件の男に、

『貴下は、拳闘と試合するんですか？それとも柔道とやるんですか？望みは何力

ですが』

『相手は何力でも構ひません』

『それぢや拳闘と試合して下さい、オイ君、誰れがいゝだらう？』

"Oh no, I forgot to ask him the most important question! Does he want to go against a boxer? Or does he want to have a match with a Judo practitioner? I got distracted and completely forgot, how embarrassing."

Hearing this the manager hurriedly turned to the man in question and asked,

"Do you want a fight with a boxer? Or do you want to have a go at a Judo practitioner? Which would you prefer?"

"Either opponent is fine with me."

"Very well then, you will be fighting a boxer...Hey, you! Who do you think would be best?"

"Seems like George would be a good match. Once he gets going it doesn't matter if his opponent is a Judo practitioner or whatever, he's going to win."

"That sounds good." The manager said, before turning to the man and asking his name. He then quickly had a poster put up announcing the next bout.

"Boxer George versus a sudden challenger Motobe Asamoto."[27]

Pinan Yondan no Kamae
Pinan Fourth Level Stance

"Hey, there is the *Tobi-iri,* the guy that just walked in off the street to challenge someone!"

"Just walked in off the street? This is gonna be good! Ok, looks like his opponent...is a boxer named George. The guy that just walked in is Motobe Asamoto. Amongst boxers George is known as a tough fellow, but does anyone know anything about this new guy? Motobe Asamoto, a challenger off the street? I get that he just signed up to fight today but what is he, a Judo practitioner?"

"Well he's Japanese so it's likely he's a Judo practitioner."

Just as this conversation was wrapping up the first signal sounded

---

[27] Motobu Choki's name is written correctly in Kanji however a more standard Japanese style of reading is given. It is not clear if this indicates Motobu Choki altered his name when he entered this duel or the publisher wrote the incorrect reading for his name.

For reasons unknown, the illustration depicts Funakoshi Gichin and not Motobu Choki.

and the pair walked out into the ring. On one side was the boxer George, who the crowd was already familiar with. George was a tall, fat man, and a famous boxer however his opponent, who had just walked in off the street, was another matter. The older fellow who had just walked in off the street was a rugged looking man who was a bit fat and stood about 5 Shaku 4 Sun tall, 164 centimeters/ 5'4." By the looks of him he was about fifty-two or fifty-three years old. Seeing how vital and animated George's body was the Japanese man seemed to be rather small and pathetic in comparison.

"He's got some years on him in my opinion."

"Not putting on gloves, I guess he's a Judo guy."

"He doesn't seem like the kind of guy who would suddenly show up to a martial arts tournament and apply for a fight on the spot. I wonder what his story is."

"You get 'em gramps!"

Meanwhile the crowd had reacted the opposite of what was expected, half the shouts were teasing the sudden challenger. Thus with insults flying the second signal sounded and the two combatants moved quickly apart from each other.

George immediately took *Tsuki no Kamae*, a fighting stance with both gloves moving in a quick up and down rhythm, repeatedly darting out and back. On the other hand, the rough looking fellow going by the name Motobe stood with his left arm held above his eyes as if he were trying to look at something in the distance and his right hand near his right cheek and his hips firmly lowered. The audience responded to his stance by shouting things like,

"Eh? What is that all about, it looks like he's getting ready to dance?"

"No idea, the way he's holding his hands resembles Kenbu, sword dance."

"This strange fellow just jumped into the ring out of nowhere!"

The people backstage were also scratching their heads over how the on the spot challenger was standing when one of them, a Judo practitioner, after studying Motobe's Kamae for a time suddenly shouted, "Ah-ha! Karate!"

The man standing beside him parroted him, "Karate?!"

"Hm, yes, it is definitely Karate."

"What is Karate?"

「挌闘なもの
が飛出したも
のや！」
などと観衆はとり
どりの評、樂屋の人々も
思はぬ飛入りに、首を出し
て見てゐたが、その中一人の
柔道家は、本部の構へを見てゐ
るうちに、思はず、

『ア！
唐手！』と叫んだ。

『唐手ッて？』

『ウム、たしかに唐手だ！』
鸚鵡がへしに他の一人は訊いた。

再び解せぬやうに問返へしたのも
無理はない、今日と雖も、唐手と云
つただけでは、何う云ふ武技である
か、まだ廣く世に知られてゐないに
相違ない。卽ち筆者は、一言唐手な
るものに就て説明しておかなければ
なるまい。

唐手はこれ琉球特有の武技、今より約三百年の昔慶長
十四年、琉球島が島津氏の爲めに平定せられて以來、武器と云

ふ武器を一切
取上げられた
ところから、
止むにやまれ
ぬ防禦の手段
として、武器
を帶びず、ま
た徒手空拳を
以て敵にあた
るべく工夫せ
られた獨特の
武技、自然、
その技に至つ
ては、一擊に
して敵を死に
至らしむると
云ふ稀代の代
物、これをわ
が古來の柔術
や、最近の

道に比すれば、投げこそ少ないが、その手足を唯一の武器と
して、突き手に蹴り手に、一擊直ちに敵を斃すの黙に於ては
は、寶に驚くべき魔力を有してゐる。されば昔より琉球に於い

るが、うち見たるところ、五十二三歳の朴魯漢、見るからに生生灣剌たるギョージに比しては、餘りにその容姿がクスブリ過ぎてゐる。

分、口々に與太を飛ばしてゐるうちに、第二の合圖は鳴つた。二人の試合者はサツと離れた。

ギョージはぶふまでもなく突きの構へ、兩手のグローブを刻みに動かしつゝ突き手のハツミをくれてゐるが、一方本部と名乘る朴魯漢は、遠方を眺めるが如く顰し、右手は依賴に近くあげてグツと腰をおとした身の構へ。

『ハテ、何んですやろ、踊みたやうにして』

『分らん、蠍舞みたいな手つきや』

『袋をしないぞ、柔道家かな?』

『飛入りするやうた柄でもなささうちやないか、何うしたんだらう?』

『銃さんしつかりやれ!』

觀衆は、豫期に反した懲入りに、からりアテがはづれたやうに、聲媛も何うやらひやかし戦

『えらう年寄りやな』

It is not surprising that the questions and answers went back and forth like this, in a manner that didn't result in a clear answer, since even today not many people are familiar with the martial art known as Karate.

I think it would be beneficial if the I were to explain what Karate is to my readers.

Karate is a martial arts system unique to Ryukyu. About three hundred years ago during the fourteenth year of Keicho (1609,) the Shimazu clan sought to subjugate the people of the Ryukyu islands by collecting all swords and weapons. Thus, in order to have a self-defense martial art that would be effective against an aggressor they developed a unique method through trial and error. This naturally developed into *To-Shu Ku-Ken*, an Unarmed and Empty Handed, method that did not rely on carrying a weapon on your person.

This unique system would allow you to kill an opponent with a single blow. If compared to the old martial art of Jujutsu, or the more recent Judo, the number of throwing techniques are fewer however the hands and feet are incredible weapons. Whether you are talking about their striking techniques and kicking techniques, the fact that one strike can topple an opponent shows that Karate practitioners possess and almost otherworldly power.

However, long ago in the Ryukyu islands there was a fear of people using Karate for evil purposes thus teachers would not accept a person as a student until after they evaluated their character. However even if a teacher agrees to instruct you, you are not allowed to train in public and can only train at home in a room closed off to others. While nowadays he serves as the president of the Shobu Kai, when the great practitioner of Karate Jutsu, Funakoshi Gichin, was a child he kept the lessons he learned from his teacher a closely guarded secret. Before training he was made to promise before his ancestors that he would never use any of the techniques he was taught for violence or intimidation. However, now these techniques being made public and are even being employed as an exercise method in schools is an extremely recent development.

The stance that members of the audience thought resembled a movement from Kenbu, sword dance, is actually from the Karate school Shorin Ryu. It is called Pinan Yondan no Kamae. You use your left hand to block or sweep away the opponent's attack and then your right hand is immediately employed to feed the opponent a thunderous fist to the face. Thus, the despite the fact that the man's face appeared old he stood perfectly in Kamae, without the slightest gap in his defenses. Just looking at the energy the man projected was liable to make you nervous since he seemed to be an altogether different person.

"You can't let your guard down!" shouted the Judo practitioner who had previously shouted "Karate!"

The two powerful warriors were both ready for whatever came next.

Hirate Uchi
A Face Slap

"Challenger just off the street! Go get him!"

"George go after him!"

However, George being a famous and skilled boxer, was able to determine his opponent did not have the slightest weak point in his Kamae that would enable his punch to enter... So, George didn't seem to be able to attack as if he was surprised and thinking, "What's this?!" George just continued to jab out with both arms. If he found an opening he would jump in and attack, however his opponent continued to stand perfectly still in his stance, not making the slightest movement.

It seemed as if the Karate practitioner's stance was pressuring George who was now breathing heavily with a *Hah, Hah!* sound. If he kept up that pace he was going to become tired and his opponent would take advantage of him. This was out of the question so George decided to draw his opponent out.

So, he employed a certain boxing technique to draw an attack. He quickly raised first one hand as if he was going to strike with it and then the other as if he were going to jab with it all the while slowly, slowly closing the distance. However, George's opponent did not react to his attempts to draw him in and instead remained as inscrutable as before, completely unmoving.

り思ひ切つて一歩二歩、進み寄ると見る間に、ヤッ！と身を
すくめて遉二無二の突き、敵の面部目がけた巨彈の沛發！ア
ワヤと思ふ一瞬間、パツくと閃めく本部が卒手、はじめの遉
りの體勢更に崩さず小手さき怜く怜な
く宗ボーンと敵の巨彈をハネ返へして
了つた。

『何を！』

今はチョージも捨身、突きに繋ちに
巨彈と云ふ巨彈に打ちかゝつて行つた
が、相手は更に動ぜず、左手一閃、ボ
ボーンとハネ返され、攊ひハジカれて
齒が立たない。が、チョージもさるも
の、危いッ！と見るや、サツと身を顧
へして、もとの位置、更らに敵の虛を
かがつてゐたが、ハッ！ハッ！と
云ふ彼れにも似合はぬ始のやうな息
遣ひは、餘程に疲れたものと相見えた。
これに引きかへ相手の本部は依然たる
體勢、動ぜざると山の如く、その息遣
ひも極めて静かだ。

『チョージ、何うしたんだ！』
一樂屋の人々も氣が氣でない、犬晴し、一團の御大たるチョー
ジともあらうものが、この一老蕉に手が出ないとは何うしたと

だ、と、唐手の怜物たるかを知らない沛中は、

『遠慮は無用！行け、チョージ！』
と躍氣となる、觀衆はたゞ呆氣にとられるばかり、こゝにチ
ョージは、一氣に勝敗を決しよ
うと決心したものゝ如く、やお
ら右手を大きく開いたと見る間
に、ツツッと二三歩、大股に詰
め寄りざま面部の撃ち手、
宙にウナツて振飛

『アッ！』
本部の面上微塵と思ひきや、
鏘として鳴る鐵腕の響き！本
部は、左の卒手に、振飛び來た
る敵の右手を一捩強くパツと上
ね返へす、途端に伸びる腰の構
へ、それと間髮をいれず右の卒
手、電光の如く突出せば敵の心
上臺として靜あり、アッ！と
云ふ間に、チョージは、口鼻の
間を、卒手にズズーンと突き上げられた。チョージの軆は、大ぎの瞬間、さながらボクトツ
の如くドタリと打倒れて了つた。

唐手の構へ　富名百氏（右）　本部氏（左）

氏部本（左）氏鎮名富（右）へ構の手唐

Motobu Choki (left) and Funakoshi Gichin (right) in Karate Kamae

At this point George was boiling over with desire to strike his opponent, thinking, "What do I have to do to get him to react?" as he edged forward again first one step then two before suddenly with a shout of *Ya!* George tucked his body and charged recklessly forward, throwing two giant swings aimed at his opponent's face.

The attacks raced towards the Karate practitioner's face, but as they were about to make contact Motobe reacted like lightning. Without disturbing his stance, he quickly, and apparently effortlessly, knocked aside George's giant punches with a quick *Bish Bash!* using his open hand.

"What was that!?"

George, despite advancing well into his opponent's striking range and throwing huge punches that seem to rocket towards the Karate practitioner, didn't cause his opponent to move in the slightest. Instead his left hand whipped out like a bolt of lightning and with a *Bish Bash!* Had knocked George's punches aside, meaning George's gambit couldn't take bite out of Motobe's defenses.

However George was a shrewd athlete and thought to himself, "Better watch out!" as he saw Motobe's reaction. He darted back out of the way, returning to his original position to evaluate his opponent's strategy. However, by now George was huffing and puffing with his breathing coming in gasps that sounded like *Hah! Hah!*, as he uncharacteristically burned through his energy reserves. He was beginning to look tired. On the other hand his opponent, Motobe, was in the same stance he began in, as unmoving as a mountain. His breathing was extremely quiet.

"Hey! What's the matter George!?"

The people backstage had no idea what was going on. Why wasn't giant George, the brilliant fighter, who was always grandiose, taking any swings at the rough looking old man?

ても、唐手の籔腕せられるを恐れ、先づその人と慴らを見抜か
ない以上、演子と毫もなか／＼に致へ、よしまたこれを辯ふ
にしても公開の席上などでは一切やらず、さそかに自分の家の
宗に謝ちをもつて傳授するよ云ふ慣、現在沖繩縣尚武會丈に
して唐手術の大家たる高名な腰養珍氏な

その幼少時代、師について習つ
た卽には、極めて秘密に、雨かも一
切爆暴な手投には用ひないと云ふ宣誓
を親先の前にしてから習ひはじめた
程、この技が漸く世に分けられ、沖
繩縣下の學校などに、運動として採用
せられたのは極めて最近の事で、食、観
祭が、躬舞みたいだと云つた姿勢は、
これぞ唐手にかける少林流、ピンアン
四投の構へ、左手に敵の攻撃を受け拂
ふが否や、右手の拳殻を食はすもの、
ビタリと構へたたその醴貌は、見るく
なく、老人じみたその醴貌は、見るく
緊張し來つて、さながら別人の如く輝やく。
『油斷は出來んゼッ！』と
ざきに『唐手！』と看破した柔遺家の一人は、思はずさう
言。
さばれ、兩者の膝觸愁と鳴るところ、そこに捲起る風霪や果

一拳五分横を瀨割の卵く打つたり由田展織氏

きにあらず、この上は誘き出しにかゝられたらないと沈心し
たか、拳鬪一流の誘ひ、兩手をサツと騙しつゝ、襟つが如く突
く、が如く小剞みに馴かしながら、ヂリヂリと攻め寄せて行く。
が、構へは更にその誘ひに乘つて來ず、依然として微動だもし
ない、愈々業を煮やしたヂョージは、えゝ、これまで！とばか

『ヂョージ、猶けッ！』
佛しヂョージも背に聞こえた
拳鬪家遊が敵の構へに、打込ん
むべき寸毫の際もないのを見る
とこれは！と驚いたかたか
なかに攻撃しない、たや雨殺に
ハズミをくれて、隙があれば
飛掛らんとしてゐるが、敵はぴ
タリと構へたまんま、微動だも
しない。その醴軟に腰せられた
か、ヂョージは刻々に息をハズ
マせ、バックく！と云ふ烏使、
この儘に疲れて了つては知ち
敵に乘ぜられる、かくて果つ

氏雄辰田山たつ割打く如の餅煎を板分五擊一拳鐵

Yamada Tetsuo breaks five boards with Tekken Ichi Geki, one blow with iron fist, as if they were Senbei, Japanese rice crackers.[28]

---

[28] Yamada Tetsuo seems to have set the boards up on an upside down Go board.

While the manger backstage shouted, "Don't hold back! Go George!" the spectators seemed to be in a state of shock.

George had apparently decided to bring this fight to a conclusion with one great attack. He drew his right fist back and took two or three large steps forward, closing the distance between himself and his opponent. With his entire body behind it, he launched a powerful right punch aimed for his opponent's face. He swung so hard that he was nearly flying through the air.

At the sight of this the crowd gasped, "Ah!"

It seemed as if Motobe's head was going to be shattered into dust. However, the blow was interrupted with the ringing of his iron arm. Motobe used the palm of his left hand to defect the George's right punch with a *Bam!* and, almost in the same instant, he leaned, extending his body forward and transitioned to an attack in an interval of time so narrow not even a hair could fit in the gap. The Karate practitioner slammed his palm up into George's face. The blow struck like a bolt of lightning and with a shout of *Ah!* George was hit in the mouth and nose. Before he could so much as cry out, Motobe's palm slammed into the spot between George's mouth and nose, and drove upward.

Though this was a strike with the palm, it struck in the vital point between the mouth and nose. In the next second George tipped back and fell to the ground as if a wooden sword had fallen over. The spectators were astounded…. and the only sound that came out of their mouths was a collective *Waaaa!* as they looked at George, who was laying on the ground not moving. Suddenly, someone from behind the scenes shouted, "Get the doctor!" and several people ran out to offer assistance to the unconscious George.

"What a frightening old fellow that guy is."

The crowd was so stunned by the way the match concluded they could barely string two words together.

観衆は思はずワッ……と歓聲をあげたが、チョージは倒れた
まゝもう動かない。

「ワレ！介抱！」

楽屋の人々は、その聲に怯り出て、悶絶し
たチョージを擔ぎ入れた。

「恐ろしい爺さんやたァ！」と

観衆は、除りの事に呆氣にとられ、二の句がつけなかった。

○柱も凹む

一失態ながら、貴下のは唐手ですネ？　さきに、唐手と氣附い
た武道家の一人は、その試合の終了後、さう云ぶって本部氏に訊
いた。

「御存じですか」

と、彼には、本部氏の拳を見せてくれと云ぶったが、その拳を
見るに及んで、庭に驚いたには、このげんこつ、ギュッと振れ
ば文字通りさゝえ！　その皮膚は石、全く石同然、打てばカチ

「唐手の噂はかねぐ〜聞いてゐましたが

「四虚程これでは、水手でも堪らん！」

と、楽屋一同が、この飛入り者のげんこつに驚いたも道理、
琉球の唐手を習ふ程のものは、はた薄板に、錢
口、右拳を打ちつけつゝ、突き手の力を捻り出して
居るから、厚さ一寸三分の板などとは、そのげんこつに一撃す
れば、さながら砲力でも用ひてたゞ割つたやうに、バラリと割

れて了ふ。況してこの本部興基氏は、琉球の名門本部御主に生
れて、唐手の戦闘術即ち巷戦の強弱に至つては、理に誰れも知らも
のもない大國基、其のげんこつの自點をコツンと叩く柱に打ち
つければ、柱の方がベコンと凹むと云ぶのだから、若し人あつ
て、そのげんこつに力いつぱい一撃されんか、骨は忽ち微塵に
碎けて了ふのだ。チョージが忽ち微塵に、チョージが忽ち
その水手の一撃に、倒れたのも無

理はない。

「琉球の唐手！」

ソム、あの小さな島にそんな隠れたる武技が
あつたのかなァ！　ちつとも知らなかった！　成程、あゝげん
こつ一つありさへすれば、何の武器も要るまい。イヤあのげん
こつこそ髪通自在、實に恐るべき武器だ、それにしても、人間

も窮すると、さらい主を天才するものだ！

と、楽屋の人々は、口々にさうぶつて感嘆したのである。(をはり)

野牛を打ち殺す

唐手は身體全體を武器とする必要はない、拳は拳撃、据伏、鐵板裏
に打ちつけて鍛へ、足は鐵や裉の下駄を穿いて蹴る力を出す。
手備への大家である宮名腰義珍氏の先輩鈴木と六人の姐と、琉球八重
山で野牛の暴れるのを『こいつ！』とばかり側の鐵拳を臨天に食はせ
ると、進む騒然の暴れ野牛もクルくくツと廻つて死んで了つたと云ふ。實
に、拳の強さは一つの鐵拳とも云ぶべく、一時この拳は法律上凶器

と極稍に見なされた程である。

Hashira mo Hekomu
Can Even Dent a Wooden Pillar

Following the fight, the Judo practitioner, the one who had first identified Motobe as a Karate practitioner said, "Sorry, can I ask, do you do Karate?"

"Do you know about Karate?" replied Motobe.

"For some time now there have been a lot of stories circulating about Karate."

The Judo man asked to see Motobe's hands. When he looked at them he was even more surprised. When Motobe made a Genkotsu, hands squeezed into fists, they resembled turban shells! The skin on his hands was like stone, absolutely like stone. Without a doubt striking something with that hand would cause the target to ring.

"I understand now. With a hand like that, even an open-handed strike isn't something a person can endure."

All the back of the house people then asked to see the hands of the man who had just walked in off the street and defeated a boxer. They were surprised but understood that in the Ryukyu islands Karate practitioners train their right fists daily by striking Makiwara, Mokuban (wooden boards) or Teppan (iron boards) continually in order to toughen the hand and increase the power of their strikes. Due to this a Karate practitioner can use his Genkotsu to smash through a board 1 Sun and 2 or 3 Bun, 3.6 cm/1.4 inches, thick with one strike. The board will shatter apart as if electricity has been used.

Mr. Motobe Asamoto was born into the famous Motobe Family in Ryukyu and became a powerful man due to training Karate Sento Jutsu, Karate Battle Techniques, in other words he learned Jissen, practical combat skills. In his hometown there is no one that does not know of this formidable man.

It is said that even with a light strike with his fist, the knuckles of which are covered with mounded calloses, will dent a wooden column. Thus any person on the receiving end of a punch thrown full power with that fist would have their bones completely disintegrated. Thus it was not surprising that George was knocked unconscious by an open handed strike from such a hand.

"Ryukyu Karate! Hmm, I cant believe this martial art came from such a small country! I had no idea. It makes sense though, if you have a fist like that, you don't really need any weapons. Plus that

Kenkotsu, fist, combined with that ability to adapt to any fighter and move with complete freedom?! Truly a frightening weapon! When humans are put in a tough situation they can truly come up with some marvelous things!"

This and other such excited comments were made by the tournament staff.

End

Translator's Note:

Sazae, or turban shells, can be written in Kanji as Sazae 拳螺 "fist snails." The snails can be eaten as sashimi or grilled in the shell.

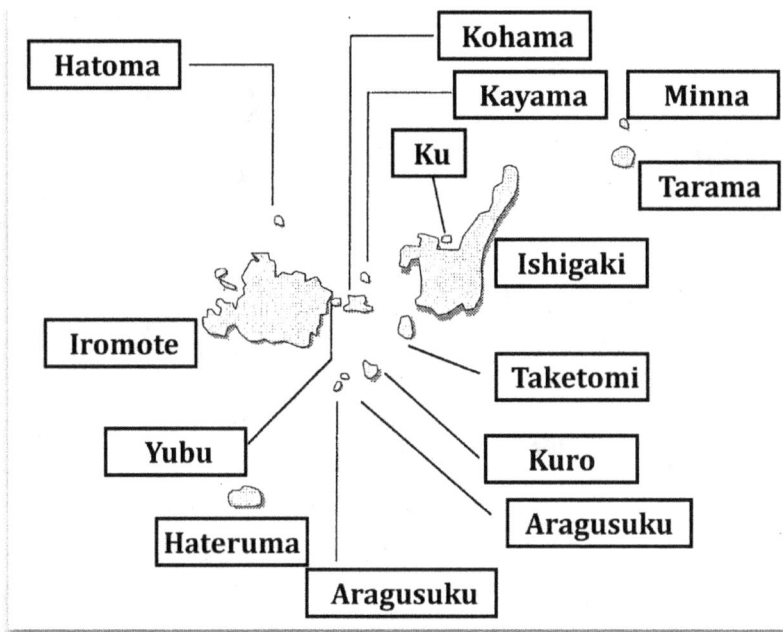

The Yaeyama Island Group

Noushi wo Uchi Korosu
Striking a Wild Cow Dead[29]

In Karate the entire body is used as a weapon. The fist is hardened by striking Makiwara, Sue Tawara (straw bale,) Teppan (iron plate) and so on. On their feet Karate practitioners wear iron or stone Geta and practice kicking to develop power.

Funakoshi Gichin, currently one of the most famous active Karate Jutsu practitioners, had a man senior to him named Hachimine. In the Yaeyama island group in Ryukyu, a wild cow was rampaging around. Hachimine confronted the animal and shouted, "Come on!" and struck the beast with his Tekken, iron fist. It is said that after the blow the wild cow that had been mad with rage wobbled around before falling down dead. Truly an example of a fist capable of inflicting incredible damage. At one point his fists were considered to be legally the same as a weapon.

---

[29] This was a small paragraph attached after the story of Motobu Choki's duel.

家憲物語
Kaken Monogatari
昭和 5
Showa 5 (1930)

唐手習得の心得

武士が帶刀の代りに稽古した

本 部 朝 基

傳説によると唐手は古來支那において行はれてゐたのを達磨大師が精林寺で禪定修業をして

ゐる時、どうも山奧のお寺のことゝて、猛獸がノコ〳〵現れて來て行を妨げて困る。そこで大

師はこの唐手を用ひて、この等の猛獸を追拂つた。この時大師今まで散漫に傳へられてゐた種

々の型を綜合大成して唐手の基礎を作つたと傳へられてゐる。何故、琉球においてこの術が獨

特の發達を遂げたか、琉球が支那と近く古くから交通してゐたといふ地理的關係もあらうが、

薩摩の島津家によつて征服せられ、帶刀を禁ぜられてから、武器なくして敵を倒すこの術が異

Karate Shutoku no Kokoroe
Things to Remember When Training Karate

Samurai Warriors Substituted Training Karate for Carrying a Sword

Regarding Motobu Choki

According to legend, Karate was trained in ancient China. When Daruma Daishi, the Bodhidharma, was residing at Shorinji Temple, he found that since the monks were doing their intensive training in the remote mountains, they were frequently being attacked by wild creatures. The great teacher Daruma used Karate to get rid of the dangerous wild animals. It was at this time that the great teacher collected all the innumerable scattered teachings and consolidated them into one comprehensive system. This then formed the Kiso, foundation of Karate.

So why then did this become particularly developed in the Ryukyu islands? One reason is close geographic distance. From ancient times the Ryukyu Kingdom has traded with China. Later when the Shimazu Clan that ran Satsuma Domain conquered and occupied the Ryukyu islands they banned the carrying of swords, thus the ability to defeat an enemy barehanded became unusually developed in these islands.

家憲物語

様の發達をしたのだといはれてゐる。本部氏は琉球王家侯爵と同族で本部城の城主であつた人の子孫である。この術は前記の如く武士が帶刀代りに稽古したものであるから帶刀そのものゝ如く普及され、武術の師範家みたいに家元といふのがない。名人といはれた人をあげると佐久川、西牟田、城川等の人々が語り傳へられてゐる、

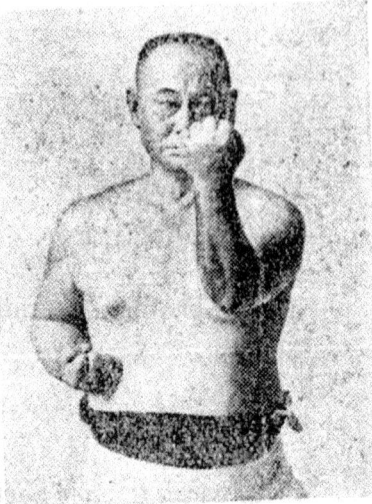

さて、この試合であるが、ボキシングのやうには行かず、眞劍にやると相手を即死させるといふ結果になつてしまふ。左右の手足、ひぢ、すね、指等とあらゆる部分を活動させるのであつて、手は拳をかためて正面攻撃をやり、掌で横なぎして頸動脈を切つたり、手足の筋を切つたり、足は蹴上げ、ひぢは脇腹、すねはこう丸、指は眼、眉間と處かまはず攻め立てるのだから物凄い。しかし、技量の伯仲した名人同士の試合になると、かやうな危險はなくなるさうである。といふのは雙方とも「受けはづしの手」がシツカリしてゐるので容易に突きがはいらぬ、よしはいつても一度は受け外されてゐる

228

The Motobu family is related to the Sho family of kings in Ryuku and Motobu Choki is a descendent of the head of Motobu Castle.

As was previously mentioned, this art was done by warriors as an alternative to carrying a sword and it spread to all warriors just like wearing a sword usually would. However, unlike in Kenjutsu there was no Shihan-ke, or family of professional instructors that were employed directly by the emperor or Shogun and inherited their position. There was also no Iemoto, or primary family of martial arts instructors.

Some of the famous names in this art that you hear stories about are, Sakukawa, [30] Nishimuda, Kusukawa.

With regards to Shiai, or bouts, they are not done like in boxing matches, since in a true fight the opponent would be instantly killed.

The hands and feet are employed along with the elbows, shins and fingers in various ways against every part of the opponent's body.

The hands are squeezed into fists and used to strike the face. The palm is used to attack with attack with sweeping horizontal strokes, cutting into the carotid arteries, or to cutting into the tendons of the hands and feet.

They use their legs to kick upward and their elbows to strike to the sides of their enemies. Even more dramatic is how they use the shins to strike Kogan, the groin, while the fingers attack the eyes, Miken, the spot between the eyebrows, or any other place on the body.

However, if it is a fight between two well-known Karate practitioners of equivalent skill, the danger completely evaporates. The reason for this is both practitioners are accurately employing *Uke-Hazushi no Te*, Blocking and deflecting techniques, So actually landing a blow is no easy matter. So it is not easy for them to land a blow.

---

[30] Kanga Sakugawa (1786 ~1867.)

から急所をそれるとか、力が抜けるとかするのださうである。突き手は單に突くだけでなく、突いてねぢ込むやうにするので、表面より内部に強くあたる。このねぢ込みの力の入れ具合で表面から何枚目と指定して積み重ねた瓦を割ることも出來る。俗に一年目に殺すやうに突くのを一年殺し、二年目に死ぬやうに突くのを二年殺しといつてゐるのもこんなところからいひはやされたのであらう。稽古は卷ワラといふものを作り、これを突き、この卷ワラがハネ返つて來るのを外すのであるが、突く基本姿勢は『八文字立で八字形に爪先を開き、兩手を自然のま丶垂れ、腰をすゑ、下腹にウンと力を入れる』と教へてゐる。これが出來上つて、組手即ち實戰の色々な突き手、うけ外しの手を研究するのであるが、相手を選んで色々に苦心し、今日まで殘されてゐる型以外にその人々に適當する新型を考案してもい丶のであつて、定型なるものはないとされてゐる。こ丶に最も尊重されてゐるのは敏捷であることである。次に唐手習得の心得を抜萃すれば、

一、唐手は弱い方に力を盡し、左手を多く役立たせるやうに心掛く

一、朝洗面すると同じく唐手練習者は練習が必須の條件である是非朝夕二回、終世續けね

229

You may think you are going to land a blow, but it is immediately blocked so. The energy is deflected away from the Kyusho, vital point you were aiming for. Since the power has been taken out of your attack, you only just get a glancing blow.

A Tsuki , or straight punch, does not describe your arm simply moving forward, rather you are twisting as you drive your fist in, which delivers more force to the inside of the body rather than the surface.

For example, depending on the way you strike with this twisting action, you can determine in advance which roof tile in a stack of tiles you are going to break.

There is a colloquial term for when striking a person so that they die within a year is called *Ichinen Koroshi*, Kills Within a Year. If you strike a person so that they die within two years, it is called *Ninen Koroshi*, Kills Within Two Years. It is likely that these terms originated with the above mentioned way of striking.

For training, Karate practitioners make a thing called Makiwara and strike it. When the Makiwara rebounds, they deflect that.

Karate practitioners are taught "The basic stance is called Hachimonji, eight shaped, a way of standing with the toes of the feet pointed diagonally outward like the shape of the Kanji *Hachi* 八 or eight. The arm should hang down naturally and the hips are lowered. Put power in your lower abdomen with a shout of *Un!*

After you learn this, you will practice Kumite, paired training, which means Jissen, a real fight. Kumite training means you will be learning how to block and deflect. However, depending on the opponent you select, you might be in for a rough time.

In addition to the Kata that had been handed down, some practitioners have developed new kata to focus on certain points so the Kata that Karate practitioners train are not fixed. The most important aspect to focus your attention on is moving quickly and nimbly.

Next is an extract of the most important lessons in Karate.

- In Karate, you should focus your power on the weakest points. You should ensure you are developing your left hand so that it is able to be useful to you

本部朝基・MOTOBU CHOKI

家憲物語

ばならぬ。

一、武の観念を忘れず、謙譲克己の精神で終始せねばならぬ。

一、精神の統一、鍛練を習練し實戦には相手と對立したゞけで、相手の心を見抜くやうにせねばならぬ

この道においても矢張、精神の修練は第一におかれ、謙譲の徳はたゝへられてゐる。

（寫眞は本部朝基氏）

230

- Just as you wash your face every morning, it is essential that Karate training become a daily habit. Training should be twice a day, morning and night, and continue until the end of your days.

- Do not forget the meaning of Bu, martial arts. You should endeavor to maintain modesty and self-discipline.

- Your mind and spirit learn how to forge the body through training and when you are facing off against an opponent in a real fight, you must learn to see through to your opponent's true intent, his true nature.

For those following this path, the most important thing is rigorously train your mind while following the path of modesty.

(The photograph is a picture of Mr. Motobu Choki.)

空手研究 第 1 輯
Karate Kenkyu Dai Ichi Go
Karate Training Volume One
昭和 9
Showa 9 (1934)

空手一夕譚

本部朝基

◇大道館道場に本部先生をお訪ねして、空手についていろ〳〵の御話しを拝聽した。以下文責は記者に在り。(大道館は本鄉區田町二五番地)

糸洲先生と平安

私は子供の時から武藝が好きで、多くの先生について研究したが、糸洲先生について稽古したのは私が十七八歳から二十四五歳位までの七八年間です。糸洲先生は、はじめ浦添の澤岻に居られたが・那霸の仲島大石前に轉居しられたが、それから識名に移り更に伊江男爵別莊に越され、晩年は中學校下に住んで居られた。

糸洲先生が中學校下に住んで居られる頃、私は一日先生をお訪ねして、いろいろ武藝談や世間話をして居た。丁度そこへ學生が二三人訊ねて来て、席を先生に加はつて話して居るうちに、糸洲先生は學生に向つて型を所望された。以前に私がならつた「チャンナン」といふ型によく似て居るが多少違つて居るところがある。「何とふ型ですか?」と學生にたづねて見ると『ピンアンの型です』とのことであつた。

間もなく學生諸君は帰ったので・先生にむかつて私は質問した。

「私はチャンナンといふ名で習ひ、型も今のとは違ふやうですが、どういふわけですか?」

するると糸洲先生は

「その頃とは型は多少違つて居るが・今では學生のやつたあの通りの型に決定して居る。名稱もみなが平安がよいといふから、若い者達の意見通りにさうしたのだ」

とのお話しであつた。此型は糸洲先生の創始られたものだが、先生一代の間に右のやうな變化があつた。

武士長濱と糸洲先生

糸洲先生は武士長濱が辻前毛に居られた頃に長濱先生について稽古されたことがある。

長濱先生は糸洲先生よりは一つしか年長ではなかつたが、糸洲先生は先輩として又先生として長濱先生を尊敬し

—(20)—

Karate Isseki Hanashi
An Evening Spent Taking About Karate With Motobu Choki

I paid a visit to the Daido Kan, Motobu Sensei's Dojo and talked with him about many different things. The writer takes full responsibility for this article. (The Daido Kan is located in Number 25 Hongo, Tamachi Tokyo.)

Itosu Sensei and Pinan

From a young age I have enjoyed martial arts and studied with many different teachers. I first started training with Itosu Sensei around the time I was seventeen or eighteen years old, until the time I was twenty-four or five, so a total of about seven or eight years. At first Itosu Sensei lived in the Takushi section of Urasoe however he later moved to a place in Naha right in front of *Nakashima Ufu Ishi* one of the "Large Stones of Nakashima." He then moved to Shikina before moving to Iiudon Nuharuyaa, a villa owned by Baron Ie. In his final years he lived under a junior high school.

When Itosu Sensei was living underneath the junior high school, I paid him a visit one time. We talked about martial arts and as well as current events. At one point, two or three students came in and joined the conversation. Later on, Itosu Sensei turned to the students and asked them to perform a Kata. The Kata the students performed resembled Channan, a Kata I had learned from him before, but it differed slightly. When I asked the students, "What is the name of that Kata?" they replied, "This Kata is called Pinan."

A short while later, the students all departed and I turned to Itosu Sensei and asked him, "The Kata called Channan that I learned is different from the Kata we just saw. What is the reason for this?" In answer Itosu Sensei responded. "When I taught you that Kata, it was slightly different. However, the version the students are doing now is the version I've decided on. Regarding the name, since everyone liked the name Pinan with the Kanji 平安 that is what I decided to call it since that was what the young people wanted."

So that's the story. This Kata was developed by Itosu Sensei, however within Sensei's lifetime the above changes were made.

て居たので御二人の間は頗る仲がよかった。糸洲先生が私に向つて或る時次のやうな秘話を話されたことがある。

『武士長濱が病床に臥して、もう見込みがないと自覚したのか、或日私を枕許に呼び寄せて遺言された事がある。「糸洲君、自分はもう見込みがないから覺悟はして居るが、自分一生を省みて重大な間違があつたことに氣附いたから、君によく聞いておいてくれ。どうも自分の武術の流儀はあまりに身體を固くし過ぎたやうだこれはよく考へて見ると間違つたことである

そのために體を強固にする管が却つて弱くしたのではないかと思ひあたる節が多い。君にも體をかたくせよとばかり言つて教へて來たが、それは自分一生の體驗から、どうもよろしくないことを自覺したので、君が又其のままの流儀で弟子に傳へたら、罪だから、其點を訂正しておかうと思つたのだ」といふ長濱先生の遺言であつた』

と糸洲先生は語られた。若い人達も此話はよく味つて聞いておくがよい。

ナイフアンチ

本部師範

ナイフアンチの型で、松村先生と糸洲先生と異つてゐるところがある。ナイフアンチの中で、足を膝のところまで内側へあげて元の位置へ踏み下ろすところがある。あそこのところで兩先生の流儀が異つてゐるのだ。

松村先生の流儀は、踏みおろすときに、足を輕く平に足裏を地上におろすのだが、糸洲先生の流儀は、足のおろし方を力を入れて重く、足裏を平に下ろさず斜におろす氣持ちで、強く踏みおろす。これは右足のときも左足のときも同じことである。

次に手を胸の前面に突き出すところも兩先生のやり方が異つて居た。一つの拳を側面に腰に寄せてとり、他の拳

The Warrior Nagahama and Itosu Sensei

When Bushi Nagahama was living in the Numou section of Tsuji-mae, Itosu Sensei would train with Nagahama Sensei.

Even though Nagahama Sensei was only a year older than Itosu Sensei, Itosu Sensei respected Nagahama Sensei as his elder and teacher and the two were extremely close. One day Itosu Sensei turned to me and he relayed to me a heretofore unknown episode.

"When the warrior Nagahama was on his death bed, and there seemed no hope of his recovery, he came to a realization. Because of this he called me to his side and left me the following testament."

There's no time left for me. However, I have made my peace with that fact. Now, reflecting on my life, I realized that I made a great error and I would like to leave this testament to you. So please listen. My style of martial arts focus too heavily on toughening the body. Now that I think back on it, this was a mistake because while the goal was to make the body strong and hard, it actually seems that it weakens it. When I taught you my lessons always focused on Karada wo Katakuseyo, Toughening your body.

However based on my lifetime of experience I have come to realize that this is not the best way. Further, I feel that for you to continue teaching your students in this same manner would be criminal. I think you should correct this point.

That was Nagahama Sensei's testament to me."

The above story is what Itosu Sensei told me. I think it would be good for young people to hear this story and consider its meaning.

Naifanchi

There is a difference between how Matsumura Sensei and Itosu Sensei teach Naifanchi.

When doing Naifanchi, there is one point where you bring your foot up to knee level on the inside before placing it back down on the ground. This is the point where the teaching methods of these Sensei differ.

を胸部前面に横に突き出す型が左にも左にもある。あそこのところの拳の突き出し方が異つてゐる。

松村先生の流儀は拳を斜前に突き出すので、肘が始めと伸びてゐる。然し糸洲先生の流儀は拳を胸部に半行するやうに突き出すので時のところで角に曲げて居る。これは左手のときも、右手のときも、共に同じである。

空手と拳闘

空手を稽古して少し攻防の術をおぼえると、拳闘との仕合を問題にしたがるものであるが、それはやらぬ方がよい。空手は手でも足でも自由自在に使ふところにその価値があるのに、拳闘との立合ひになると、すべて拳闘の規則でしばられることになるから、空手としてのほんとの実力を發揮することは出來ない。研究のため拳闘と立合ひをして見たいと思ふ人は前以て幾度か其のための特別な練習が必要である。何の経験もなしに空手を知つて居るからと練習もなしに空手と立合ひをすべきではない。思はぬ不覚を取るであらう。拳闘の規則におかまひなしに、単に実力の争ひといふ事になれば、語はまた別の問題になる。空手は手足の自由な活動が生命であるから、それを慣れもせぬ規則で束縛されての他流仕合は、先づやらぬがよい。

住吉明神

新井石禅師曰く

「昔或る僧が攝州住吉の明神に詣でて『來て見ればこゝも火宅の中なるに何に住吉と人の云ふらん』と詠んだ。此處も亦無常の火に蔵はれたる危險なる姿なるに何故住吉などと云ふ呑気らしい名を附けたものかとの意です。スルト其夜神殿の中にて『善惡と思ふ心をふり捨てゝとなく住めば住吉』といふ歌の聲が聞へたとある。成にとなくとはボンヤリ遊んで居る事ではない、天地自然の道に従うて私の了見を交へぬ事です。

世に住吉明神の御託宣と云ふがあり。其の語に『我に神體なし慈悲を以て體とす。我に神力なし正直を以て神力とす。我に神通なし智慧を以て神通とす。我に奇特なし無事を以て奇特とす。我に方便なし柔和を以て方便とす』とあります、此慈悲と云ひ正直と云ひ、無事と云ひ柔和といふ、各々皆な是れ人間本性の徳です。各々此本性の徳を発揮する事が出來さへすれば、此心が即ち神なり佛なりである。」

In Matsumura Sensei's school of teaching, when you place your foot back on the ground you do so with a light step and the sole of the foot parallel to the ground. However, Itosu Sensei teaches that when placing the foot back on the ground to do so with power so your foot lands heavily. Further, you don't lower the sole of the foot horizontal to the floor, rather you lower it powerfully with a diagonal feeling. This applies to the right foot as well as the left foot.

Next, both Sensei also differ on how the hands strike straight out from the chest. One hand is drawn to your side while your other fist is held in front of your chest before striking out to the side. This part of the Kata is done with both the left and right hands. This is the part where the difference lies.

In Matsumura Sensei's style of teaching, your fist strikes diagonally forward and the elbow is almost fully extended. However in Itosu Sensei's style of teaching your fist stays parallel to the chest when striking and the elbow remains bent at an angle. It is done when you are striking with the left hand and it is done the same way when you are striking with the right hand.

Karate and Boxing

It is not uncommon for people, who after learning some offensive and defensive Karate techniques, to begin considering entering a bout against a boxer. However, this ends up being disadvantageous for the Karate practitioner, so it is best not to enter such bouts. The reason for this is that in Karate, we use both our hands and our feet freely and without hindrance, and therein lies the value of this art. However, in a boxing match you have to follow all the rules and regulations of that sport. Thus, a Karate practitioner cannot make full use of their abilities.

However, if you are a person who feels that for training purposes you would like to enter a boxing match, it is important to understand that you must undergo specialized training for a reasonable period of time beforehand.

Going into a boxing match without any experience or training related to boxing and thinking that your Karate abilities will be sufficient is not something you should do. It is important to remember this because you will end up blundering into a situation you don't understand.

Of course, if you understand the rules of boxing and are just interested in testing your abilities, then that is a whole other topic of conversation.

The free and unrestrained use of the hands and feet in Karate is the lifeblood of this art. Entering a *Ta-Ryu Jiai*, bout against a member of another school of fighting, while being constrained by rules you are wholly unfamiliar with is simply not something you should do.

空手道
Karatedo
Yabe tai Motobu no Tatakai
The Fight Between Yabu and Motobu

☆尾部対本部の闘い

師範学校教官屋部憲通氏と首里の旧家本部御殿のサールーオメー（本部朝基）との間に面白い話が残つている。屋部憲通氏は沖縄で始めて教導団という下士養成所に入団して、卒業後下士に任官、昇進して少尉当時日清戦争に従軍した人であつた。本部御殿のオメーこと本部朝基氏は封建時代士族で空手道には徹底的に練られている人である事は、世人によく知れわたつていた。この二人は互に技に甲乙がないとの話から、二人話合いの上、仕合で決したいというわけで、日を定めて決行することになつた。場所は本部御殿の表座敷、いよいよ当日になると、本部御殿の大広間の畳を全部取除き板の間にして、生命がけの闘いで勝負を決することになつた。屋部氏は青年時代から強者の噂高く、日清戦争で各地で奮戦し、空手の奥の手等を出して奮戦した経歴の持主で、抜も秀でていた。いよいよ

Yabe tai Motobu no Tatakai
The Fight Between Yabu and Motobu[31]

There is an interesting story handed down about Yabu Kantsu, at the Teacher's Training School, and the "Honorable Monkey" (Motobu Choki) from a long-established family from Shuri.[32]

Yabu Kantsu was one of the first people to entered the army non-commissioned officer school in Okinawa.[33] After successfully graduating he became a non-commissioned officer before being promoted to second lieutenant. He then saw action in the Nisshin Senso, First Sino-Japanese war (1894~1895.)

Lord Motobu the "Honorable Monkey" or Motobu Choki was a member of the warrior class during the feudal era and was well-known as a devoted practitioner of Karatedo. These two were well aware that most people considered them *Ko-Otsu ga Nai*, or so close in ability that neither could be said to be the better. Discussing this amongst themselves, Motobu Choki and Yabu Kantsu agreed to have a duel to settle the matter and they decided on a date. The fight would take place in the front parlor of the Motobu's residence. On the day of the fight, the tatami mats in the front parlor of the Motobu residence were pulled up and removed so the life or death fight

---

[31] The title writes Yabu Kentsu 屋部憲通 (1866 ~1937) as 尾部 instead of 屋部 this is likely a spelling error.

[32] Motobu's nickname was "monkey" due to his light movements. He was referred to as *Sarugozen* 猿御前 "the honorable monkey" which is pronounced *Saaraa Umee*サーラーウメー in the Ryukyu language. This book writes his nickname as Saaruu Omee. He was also referred to as *Motobu no Saru* 本部の猿 Motobu the Monkey which is pronounced *Saaruu* サールー in the Ryukyu language.

[33] In 1890, Yabu dropped out of high school and volunteered to join the army's military academy. Though there were dozens of applicants, only three were accepted.

Yabu Kentsu 屋部憲通 (1866 ~1937)

Hanagusuku Chomo 花城長茂 (1869~1945)

Kudeken Kenyu 久手堅憲由 (1869～1940)

All three of these men were students of Anko Itosu at the time.

between the fully committed warriors would take place in a large room with a wooden floor.[34]

From a young age Yabu was known as a strong warrior and during the Sino-Japanese War he engaged in fierce battle on many fronts. He was also known to have employed innumerable *Oku no Te,* high-level, Karate techniques in the course of these intense battles and was therefore extremely proficient.

Finally, the day of the fight arrived however no one was allowed to witness the event. The two faced each other with eyes glittering with martial intensity. In the time it took for the Kiai of *Toh!* to reach your ears their fists were flying. This attack was blocked and that strike was knocked aside before they jumped back. It seemed the two Karate practitioners were truly *Ko-Otsu ga Nai,* or so close in ability that neither could be said to be the better.

The fight ended several minutes later with Yabu Kentsu emerging as the winner. As it turned out, the fight and ended with neither man receiving any significant injuries and the two men parted ways in a spirit of harmony. This famous tale concludes with both men realizing the fight taught them how to further refine their technique.

One night Yabu Kentsu was travelling down the road from Naha and heading towards the Yonahara area. He was casually walking past Tsubo River when five young men appeared on the road ahead of him. They were heading away from Yonahara and walking strung across the road so Yabu would be unable to pass. The youths were clearly looking to block Yabu's passage and maybe were spoiling for a fight as a test of their strength. One of the young men intentionally bumped into Yabu and from there verbal sparks began to fly.

The youths likely had no idea that Yabu was a famous Karate practitioner and in the end one of them threw a punch. Though Yabu had no intention of fighting, the youths were clearly set on it and were planning to attack using their numbers to overwhelm their solitary opponent.

---

[34] This bout occurred after 1895, so Motobu Choku would have been about 25 and Yabu Kentsu about 30.

屋部憲通氏が師範学校に在職し、空手道の名人糸洲翁指導の下に師範学校生徒に空手道の真髄を徹底的に練成した為に、卒業生の中から優秀な達人共が輩出する様になった。修道館長の遠山寛賢氏を初め、崎浜秀厚氏、徳田安文氏、許田重発氏、城間真繁氏等が輩出した。外に摩文仁賢和氏が以上の人々と共に協力して、この道の興隆を図ったのであった。糸洲翁とならんで東恩納翁の高弟に宮城長順氏、城間恒き氏、許田重発氏等が明治、大正、昭和三代にわたって空手道の功道者であった。大正十一年頃には船越義珍氏が上京して、空手道を東京の大学生等に指導し、現在は日本空手協会の最高師範となって、その名声は高く、老いて益々元気で空手道に精進している。この人は旧藩時代からの達人安里翁並びに糸洲翁と二人の大先生の門人で、博翁朝碁氏（本部のサールー）も上京して、東洋大学共他一、二の大学生に指導の任に当っていた。この両人の過去の努力は東京で相当の実を結んだ。

（終り）

闘いの時は他人の出入も厳禁し、二人で互に眼光をきらきらと光らせて対じした。「とお」との気合が聞えるが早いか拳は飛ぶ、これをうける、そらすと又飛ぶ、なかなか二人の技は甲乙がつかなかった。が数分間の闘いの後に、遂に最後は屋部憲通氏の勝となり、とう大なる負傷もなくして結末がついて、和やかな雰囲気の中にわかれて、互に技を磨きあったという有名な話が伝えられている。

その屋部憲通氏がある晩、那覇から与那原に通ずる街道、壺川の辺をゆっくりと通りかかると、与那原方面から五人の青年が大通りを一列に広がり往来の妨げをする態度でやってくる。この青年達は自分等の腕力を試す気持であったのか、その中の一人が故意に屋部氏にぶつつかった。挙句は口争いを初めた。相手にしない屋部氏に、図にのった青年達は数を頼みにして暴力をふるうので、屋部氏はついに、向ってくる者の右手首を握ってふりまわし、路側の海の中にほうりなげた。——また一人、また一——という工合で、都合三人を海中にほうりこんだら、残りの二人は平伏してあやまったという挿話もある。

His hand having been forced, Yabu seized the right wrist of the youth who was punching at him, swung him around and threw him into the sea by the side of the road. Then a second and third youth charged Yabu in succession. Yabu threw each into the sea with an attitude of "Again?" Finally, the story ends with the remaining two youths dropped to the ground and bowed in apology.

Yabu Kentsu became an instructor at the Shihan Gakko, a teacher training school. He used the training he learned under the famous revered gentleman Itosu to ensure that the students at the teacher training school received instruction in the essence of Karatedo. Thus several of the graduates were Karate practitioners of exceptional skill. Starting with the head of the Shudokan, Toyama Kanken (1888~1966) Zakihama Hideatsu (?~?) Tokuda Yasufumi (1886~1945) Kyoda Jyuhatsu (1887~1968) Gusukuma Shinpan (1890~1954) as well as others.

In addition, Mabuni Kenwa also worked together with the above-mentioned group to help this path of martial arts to flourish. Miyagi Chojun, the top student of the revered elder Higashionna Kanryo who was on par with revered elder Itosu, along with Gusukuma Koyu (?~?)[35] and Kyoda Jyuhatsu were the great instructors of three era Meiji, Taisho and Showa.

In the 11th year of Taisho (1922) Funakoshi Gichin travelled to Tokyo and instructed Tokyo University students in Karatedo. At present he is the top instructor of the Japan Karate Association. He is very highly regarded and though elderly he is enthusiastically promulgating the essence of Karatedo. Starting in the old era when Japan was divided into feudal domains this man trained with two master instructors. The story of how Funakoshi became students of was the revered gentleman Asato and the revered gentleman Itosu is well known.

Motobu Choki (Motobu the Monkey) who Yabu Kentsu dueled with also made his way to Tokyo and taught Karate to university students at Toyo University as well as one or two other universities. No doubt both these Karate masters found that their past efforts bore fruit in while in Tokyo.

(End) The ad on the left is for Ryukyu Awamori.

---

[35] This document writes his name as 城間恆き instead of 城間恒有

日布時事
Nippu Jiji Newspaper, Honolulu, Hawaii
March 13th 1932

唐手術權威

本部朝基氏 春洋丸で來布

候補の發表をする氣だ、余は招聘に依りて來る此六日入港の春洋丸にて來布する旨來電あり、因に同氏は沖繩縣首里の素封家本部家の三男にて、少年時代より專ら唐手術の研究に從ひ唐手術に於ては日本に於ける權威者である（寫眞の本部氏）

東部に於いて數百名の子弟に唐手術を指導しつ〉ある本部朝基氏は斯道の權威者さしてその令名高く、現在東京小石川區原町にて道場を營しつ〉あるか當市の玉那霸朝長松氏の令

日本人商業會議所租税研究

當市日本人商業會議所では本日午後一時から事務所に於て租税法研究委員の集會を開き租税擁護上の研究報告に就て協議を進めた、研究の結果は近く文書さして一般に發表されることになつてゐる

けふ中央學院の父兄招待會

布哇中央學院中學校、高等女學校、高等科生

T. K. K. "Shinyo-maru"

春洋丸

Length	586 feet.
Depth	38 feet.
Breadth	63 feet.
Displacement	21,000 tons
Speed	20 knot

Karate Jutsu Keni
An Authority on the Karate Arts
Mr. Motobu Choki to Visit Hawaii Via the Ship Shinyo Maru
1932

Motobu Choki teaches Karate Jutsu to several hundred students in Tokyo. He is an authority on this art and his name is known far and wide. At present he directs training at a Dojo in the Hara Town section of Koishikawa ward in Tokyo. He was invited to Honolulu by Mr. Tamanaha Chomatsu. And is set to arrive in Hawaii on the twenty-sixth aboard the Shinyo Maru.

Mr. Motobu is from Shuri in Okinawa Prefecture. He is the third son of the Motobu family. From a young age he studied Karate Jujutsu and is considered to be an authority on Karate Jutsu. (The picture is of Mr. Motobu.)

図解空手入門
An Illustrated Introduction to Karate
Konishi Yasuhiro
1953

ナイフアンチン（内歩進）

この形は初段、二段、三段の三種がある。流儀によつては基本形とされている。

沖縄近代の拳豪と言われた、故本部朝基先生が最も得意とせられた形である。幸い先生晩年の力作として後世につたえる遺品の一つとなつたので、故先生を偲びながらこの形の寫眞を轉載して、初心者研究のよすがとする。

(1)用意──構え、で、閉足立ち、兩手を金的前に交叉させ、油断なく、前方を正視する。

(2)始め──で、ゆる／＼と靜かに顔を

(1)

Naifanchin[36]

There are three versions of this Kata, Shodan, Nidan and Sandan. Some schools of Karate use this as the Kihon Gata, fundamental technique.

This technique was a specialty of the contemporary Okinawan known as Master of the Fist, the late Motobu Choki. We are fortunate that in the last years of his life he bequeathed this tour de force to later generations. I am reminded of the late Sensei as I reproduced these photographs of the Kata to assist beginners with their training.

1. Yoh-I – Preparation. Stand in Heizoku Dachi, Feet Together, with your hands crossed in front of Kinteki, the groin. You should be looking directly forward while maintaining awareness of everything around you.

---

[36] Though the title lists this technique as Nai*fan*chin, the rest of the description uses the name Nai*han*chin.

(4)

(3)

(2)

左側方に廻して、左方を正視する。

(3)同様悠々と、靜かに顔を右側方に廻轉して、右方を正視する。

(4)靜かに、おもおもしく、氣を充たして、左足を右足に交叉させる。

(5)右足を靜かに、やゝ高めに抜いて、右側に踏み置き、並行立ちとなり、ナイハンチン立ちをして、右手をさし出す。

(6)ナイハンチン立ちを崩さず、上體だけを右方に捻轉して、左臂當り、右手掌を外部から添える。

(7)顔を正面に向け、左拳と右拳を右脇腹の前少しの點に向い合わす。

(8)氣合をこめて、顔を敏速に左側方に向け左方を正視する。

(9)依然充實した氣魄のもとに、注意深く、左方に、左拳で、拂手する。

(10)拂手した左拳を左脇腹腰の上に構えるに乗じ、右拳をよじりながら、左方に水落ち部を通つて、勢いよく突く。

(11)そのまゝ、姿勢を崩さず、右足を、左足の前方から交叉さ

324

2. Hajime – Begin! At this command slowly and silently turn your head to the left and look to your left side.

3. In the same manner, calmly and quietly rotate your face to the right, looking to the right.

4. Quietly and in a dignified manner, while brimming with energy pass your left foot over the top of your right.

(7)　　　　　　　(6)　　　　　　　(5)

(10)　　　　　　　(9)　　　　　　　(8)

5. Quietly move your right foot out from behind your left, slightly high, and step out to the right. Your feet should be parallel in Naihanchin stance as you extend your right hand out.

6. Without breaking Naihanchin stance, twist just your upper body to the right.

7. Turn your face forward, bring your left fist and right fist together under and slightly forward of your right side.

8. With intensity, rapidly turn your head to the left so you are facing your left side.

9. While maintaining the same intensity of spirt, and awareness of everything around you, use your left hand to strike with a Harai-te, sweeping fist, on your left side.

10. Bring the left fist that you struck Harai-te with to your left side, just above your waist. While twisting your right fist strike powerfully to the left, being sure the path of your fist passes across Mizo Ochi, your solar plexus.

(13)　　　　　　(12)　　　　　　(11)

す。

(12)靜かに、や丶高目に左足を抜き、左方に踏み下ろし、依然
ナイハンチン立ち、バタバタ足をせぬ事。

(13)顏を正面にむけて、前方を正視する。

(14)胸前に突き出して居る、右拳を起して、橫手となる。

(15)橫手の右拳と左腰上に構へた左拳とカイクリのようにして
右拳挊手、左拳橫手。

(16)挊手になつた右拳の手甲上に、橫手捌きをした左拳の臂部
を置く。

(17)左拳の臂部を伸ばして、裏打ちをする。

(18)裏打ちをした左拳をもとの位置にかえす。飽まで並行立ち
で腰を落したナイハンチン立ちの姿勢を崩さぬよう。

(19)充分に腰のすわり、に氣をくばつて、どつしりとせよ、正
しく顏を左方にふりむけよ。

(20)顏は左方にむけたま丶、腰に狂いが來ぬよう、左足土ふま
ずで右膝邊まで挊う。

(21)足挊いをした左足をもとの位置に踏みしめながら、腰は崩

328

11. Then, from that position, and while maintaining your posture, pass your right foot in front of your left.

12. Quietly, slip your left foot out from behind your right and step slightly high out to the left and put your foot down. You should be in Naihanchin stance as before. Your feet should not be making noise or bumping into your legs.

13. Turn your face to the front so you are facing forward.

(16)   (15)   (14)

(19)   (18)   (17)

14. You are striking directly out from your chest. Raise your right fist up. You are now in Yoko-te, side hand strike.

15. With your right fist in Yoko-te, and your left fist above your hip, rotate your right fist in a Harai-te, sweeping fist, and your left fist in a Yoko-te. This action should be done with both hands moving simultaneously and passing past each other.

16. Keeping the back of your right hand that you just executed a Harai-te with facing upward place it underneath the elbow of your left hand that you executed a Yoko-te with.

17. Extend your left elbow forward, striking Ura Ken, back fist, with your left hand.

18. After striking Ura Ken with your left fist, return it to its original position. Throughout this ensure that your feet are parallel and that your hips are lowered and you are maintaining proper Naihanchin stance.

19. While ensuring your hips are stable and your body is suffused with energy, turn and face your left in a deliberate and dignified manner.

(22)   (21)   (20)

(25)   (24)   (23)

20. While facing left and ensuring your hips do not fall out of proper alignment, pull the arch of your left foot towards your right knee in a sweeping motion.

21. While returning your left foot, which has just executed a sweeping motion, back to its original spot, And being careful not to allow your balance to falter, strike to the left with your left fist in a Yoko-te. Your left elbow should remain on top of your right fist the whole time

22. Turn to face the front and stare straight ahead.

23. Take your right fist, which is serving as a stand, and bring it down by your right side. At the same time, bring your left fist down by your right side as well, stacking it on top of your right fist. Stand with the palms of both fists facing each other.

24. While maintaining that stance rapidly turn your face to the left and stare fiercely.

25. While maintaining your balance as you have from the beginning strike out with both fists to your left, the direction which you are now facing. This is the end of the first half of this technique. The latter half of the technique begins at Photograph 5 and continues to Photograph 25. The only difference being everything is done on the other side. Finally return to the Yoh-I, ready position, shown in Photograph 1 and the technique ends.

さぬように注意して、左方に、右拳にのせたまゝ左拳を横手捌き。

⑵顔を正面に向けて、前面を正視する。

⑶臺のようになつて居る右拳を、右脇腹に構えるに乗じ、左拳もともに、右脇腹に重ね、兩手の掌部を向い合せて構える。

⑷そのまゝの構えで、素早く、顔を、左方にむけて、凝視する。

⑸充分始め同様腰を崩さないようにして、正視して居る左方に向つて双手突きをする。これで前半は終る。更に後半は（⑸圖以下から㉕圖の形式にいたる動作の反對を行つて⑴圖のような用意――構えの姿勢にかえつて終る。

その他の形について

尚其他數十種の形に就いても、一旦稿をまとめたが、あまりに膨大になるので、到底與えられた、紙面ではどうにもならぬので、他日にゆずることとし、「空手の形の種類」の項でその名稱だけでも知つておかれたい。

尚、序でに故本部朝基先生について一言すれば先生は、琉球の首里に明治三年王族の分家である本部安司の三男として出生、十六歳から空手を始め、伊知地、石峰、佐久間、國頭、泊の松茂良、松村等の諸大家に師事して研究を大成されたのである。サールと異名をとつた程この道の達人として空手を語るものの忘れてはならない特異の存在であつた。

Other Kata

[section omitted]

As far as a brief introduction of the departed Motobu Choki Sensei, Sensei was born into the Motobu family, a branch of the royal family, in the third year of Meiji in the capital of Ryukyu Shuri. He was the third son of the Motobu Anzu and at the age of sixteen began studying Karate. He studied under Ijichi, Ishimine, Sakuma, Kunjan, Matsumora of Tomari, Matsumura and other great masters of the art, and through extensive training he was able to develop into a master of the art. The fact that he had the nickname Saaru shows how he excelled at this art. Anyone who talks about Karate will acknowledge he holds a special place that cannot be forgotten.

本部朝基・MOTOBU CHOKI

続　空手道入門
Zoku Karatedo Nyumon
An Introduction to Karatedo Second Volume
大家礼吉
Ohya Reikichi
1955

本部朝基先生

喜屋武先生・富名腰先生と同年配。

本部朝桂先生（朝基先生のお兄さんで、有名な大家）と共に、幼少の頃から松村・松茂良・安里・糸洲・佐久間の諸先生について、空手の修業をされております。

本部家は本部御殿（モトブウドン）と呼ばれて貴族でしたから、そのため前記の先生方が交互に家へ教えに来られたとのことで、松村・松茂良先生等は既に老年のため、充分の稽古は出来得なかつたそうです。尚昔は名前に朝の字を許されたのは、士族の上席の部で、王家の血統といわれています。

先生は「本部のザール」といわれた程飛猿だつたそうで、那覇の辻（空手修業者が国中から出てきて、自分の技倆を試みる所で、一番塀の多い場所）の塀（六尺位の高さ）で越えられなかつたところはなかつたそうです。

Motobu Choki Sensei

He is the same age as Kyan Sensei and Funakoshi Sensei.

He and Motobu Choyu (Choki Sensei's elder brother and a famous master Karate practitioner) trained Karate from their childhood under the instruction of the following Sensei: Matsumura, Matsumora, Asato, Itosu, and Sakuma.

The Honbu family was an aristocratic family called Motobu Udoshi, the Honorable Motobus. As they were royalty the aforementioned teachers came to teach at the house in turn. Apparently since Matsumura Sensei and Matsumora Sensei were elderly, they were limited in the amount of instruction they could give.

In the old days, only upper class Samurai were allowed to have the Kanji Chou 朝 in their names, thus it is said that the Motobu family were related to the King's family. The reason Sensei is known as "Motobu Zaaru" is because he could leap around like a monkey.

本部朝基・MOTOBU CHOKI

西原町史 第 4 巻 (資料編 3)
Nishihara Choshi Dai Yon Maki
Ihono Hama no Rikishi
The Sumo Wrestler From Ihono Bay

8　伊保之浜の力士

　戦前、伊保之浜から多くの沖縄相撲の名力士が輩出した。明治の中頃、首里・那覇合同の天長節祝賀会が催され、それの余興として潟原で全沖縄相撲大会が開催された。当時、大関であった伊保之浜出身の高江洲と瓦屋の玉城との大相撲が行われ、観衆を沸かせた。そのころ、大関高江洲（一八五六年～大正期）は、沖縄相撲の力士としてつとに有名であった。

　大関高江洲のほかに、伊保之浜には米須マギー（一八五七年～一九一七年）という体重一四〇キログラム、身長六尺余の巨漢の力士がいた。本名は米須亀といい、伊保之浜屋取で山原舟を使い、薪の運搬に従事していた。

　明治二十二年、空手の達人「本部サール」こと本部朝基

Ihonohama no Rikishi
The Sumo Wrestler From Iho Bay

Before the war, a great many famous Okinawan Sumo wrestlers hailed form Ihonohama. In the mid-Meiji era (Meiji 1868~1912, Mid-Meiji 1889~1904) Shuri and Naha held a joint event celebrating the birth of the Meiji Emperor. As part of the entertainment the All Okinawa Sumo Tournament was held in the Katabaru section of Naha. At the time the Ozeki ranked wrestlers were Takaesu, who was born in Iho Bay and Tamagi who was from Kawaraya. According to *Overview of Ryukyu*, published in 1915, the crowd went wild for these two wrestlers. [37] The Ozeki ranked Takaesu (Born in 1856 and died in the Taisho Era 1912~1926) was renowned as an Okinawan Sumo wrestler.

In addition to the Ozeki Takaesu there was another famous Sumo wrestler from Iho Bay. His name was Yonesu Magii (1857~1917) and he was known for being a giant of a man standing over 6 Shaku/1.8 meters/ 5'9" tall and weighing 140 kilograms/ 309 pounds. His real name was Yonesu Kame and he was a Yaadoi "House Taker" who lived near Iho Bay and operated a Yanbaru Buni[38] which he used to transport firewood.

---

[37] A Yaadoi 屋取 (やーどぅい) "House Taker" describes the trend of poor warrior families to leave the city and take up life in the countryside. Typically families would move out of Shuri and built huts in secluded areas and cut farms out of the wilderness. They were also referred to as Kyojumin 居住人 or "dwellers." Apparently more than 130 villages were originally Yaadoi.

[38] 山原船 (やんばるぶに)These ships were used in the waters around Okinawa. The two-masted boats would transport lumber and firewood from the northern end of Okinawa to Naha and then ship rice, cloth and Shochu on the return trip. Used up until the 1950s. The northern part of Okinawa Main Island is called Kunigashira but was referred to as Yanbaru in olden times.

（一八七一年〜一九四四年）と米須マギーが対決したが、サールーはマギーに鎧袖一触たたきのめされた。米須マギーは当時沖縄一の相撲取で、彼の右に出るものは一人もなく、三十代のころ相撲を止めたといわれる。② 一説によると、米須マギーがあまりにも巨漢で無双の怪力だったので、相撲大会への出場を停止されたともいわれる。

大正期になると、東風平家一族が沖縄角界を制したといわれる。東風平朝忠（俗名チューミー）、東風平小蒲、東風平松などが有名な力士であった。その他にも伊保之浜出身の名力士として山里樽、新米須、池原などがいた。③

注① 『琉球大観』
② 『沖縄タイムス』連載「沖縄の空手武人伝」長嶺将真著
昭和五十五年一月二十三日付
③ 『琉球新報』大正四年七月九日付

In Meiji 22 (1889) the Karate master 「Motobu Saaru」 "Motobu the Monkey" or Motobu Choki (1871~1944) had a match with Yonesu Magii however Magii completely mopped the floor with Saaruu.[39]

At the time Magii was the top Sumo wrestler in Okinawa and, in fact, it seemed as if no one could best him. An article in the "Tales of Okinawa Karate Martial Artists" series from the January 23rd edition of the Showa 55 (1980) *Okinawa Times Newspaper* he competed well into his thirties. In fact, Yonesu Magii was such a giant of a man with incomparable strength that the Sumo Federation actually banned him from competition.

In the Taisho Era (1912~1926) the Kochinda Family dominated the Okinawan Sumo wrestling scene. The family produced many famous wrestlers such as Kochinda Asatada (known colloquially as Chuumii) along with Kochinda Koura and Kochinda Matsu. According to the Taisho 4 (1915) July 9th edition of the Ryukyu Shinpo Newspaper there were other famous wrestlers from Iho Bay such as Yamazato Taru, Komesu Shu and Ikehara among others.

---

[39] Gaishu Isshoku 鎧袖一触 "One touch of an armored sleeve" refers to soundly defeating an opponent. Motobu Choki would have been around 18 years old and Magii around 32 years old.

Yanbaru Boat
Collection of the Naha City Museum of History
那覇市歴史博物館 提供